If only I were with Mahatma-part -1

(purely based on the **imaginary meetings** with the great Mahatma)

(Inspired to write this book after reading the following two books on the struggle
for Independence in India –

1   WORKING A DEMOCRATIVE CONSTITUTION – a history of the Indian Experience (oxford India Paperbacks) Granville Austin ISBN 019 5656105

2   PRIME MINISTERS Nehru to Vajpayee by Janardan Thakur ISBN 81-86982-72-)8

(Note: I have included the names of Pandit Nehru Vallabai Patel and a few others in this fiction just to give a realistic view without having any other ulterior motives. I request the readers not to make any interpretation of the references or probe in-between the lines made in this fiction . I want to impress upon the readers that I only I were with Gandhiji during the freedom struggle what I could have done based on my imagination)

MILESTONE
ONE
IN POLITICS

Sabarmati Ashram, near Ahmedabad, founded by Gandhi in 1917

MEETING
ONE

"Babuji, a young man has come from Madras, wants to see you ",
one of the Ashram's inmates told Gandhi, the leader of the congress
party. It was 1930. The place was Sabarmati Ashram, in the
outskirts of Ahmedabad Gujarat.

He was going through the mails and the reviews made in the
newspapers. He looked up and requested the inmate to send the
young visitor in.

"Good morning sir" the owner of the voice was not a young man as
assessed by the inmate. Gandhi judged his age correctly-he was
not even twenty. He scanned the visitor from head to foot and with a
warm smile asked the guest to sit down on the mat very near to him,
while folding his outstretched right leg, to give room for the young
person to sit.

But the near twenty declined the offer politely, but came straight to
the purpose of his visit:

" My name is Ramachandran. But my parents call me Chandru. I am
from deep south- Pudukottai- the princely state. I am an electrical
assistant to my father. But I always think about the foreigners who
are here, living like Kings and making us to work like their slaves.
Back in my town, we have a Maharaja for the kingdom of
Pudukottai. But he is also under the control of the foreigners. I am
not happy and I hate them to be here and ruling us". There was a
pause for a few seconds- to check whether Gandhi was listening to
him. Once he was assured that the host was attentive and was
looking eagerly to hear him more, Chandru continued, with the
same staccato voice,

" Sir, Mr Gandhi, do you know, that I abused the foreigners in my
town when I was just ten, when I accompanied my father to attend
to electrical repairs to the palace where those white men lived. But
they did not understand. I did not know English well, at that time.
Then I made up my mind-I must learn their language and then go to
the palace and abuse them in English which they know well. But my

father beat me at home for my outrageous behaviour in the palace. He said that I was fortunate since no other Indian servants were present when I abused the English officer. Other wise he told my mother that I would have been in the jail. But I did not care. I learnt English from SelvaRaj, the coach driver of the palace who lives very near to my house. My father thereafter, did not take me with him, for any work, afraid of my dislike for the ruling white officers. I tried to join the group of people in my town who were against the foreigners. But they asked me to remain at home and study and come later when I grew up to be a man.

Sir, at home, my parents are against my plan to throw away the foreigners and in the town, no one allows me to join them. But I want to fight. I am not afraid of any one. In my town, how can some persons from far off countries come and order us to obey them?

When I was not knowing what to do, my friend's father, a teacher, on seeing my interest in the fight against the foreigners, one day after nine in the night, told me, in detail, about the story of the foreigners and how they came here to do business and how they had been supported by out own Kings and how they fought with those who opposed them and how they finally started ruling us. Thereafter, I went to his house everyday and wait till he was free to tell me about the developments. That was how, I came to know about you, Sir. He only advised me to go to your Ashram and meet you, in person and express my willingness to join the fight against the foreigners".
Gandhi was looking transfixed. He was just sitting and from his eyes, teardrops were flowing down. On seeing the great fighter crying, Chandru was shocked.

" Sir, I am sorry, Sir. I did not abuse you, Sir. Please do not mistake me, Sir" Chandru was pleading, by taking his hands and pressing them to his wet eyes.

The next moment, Gandhi was tightly embracing the visitor and was kissing his forehead fondly.

" My dear Chandru, you are a lion, from the caves of your own land, angry over the intrusion of stranger in your place. They have no business to be there, threatening your freedom. Our country is really fortunate to have lions like you, seeking freedom even from

4

the cub stage. Chandru, do not worry about others. I join you- you need not join me- I am eager to be with you in your fight against the foreigners. Do you understand? I will give a letter to the congress party at Madras and they would take you as a member. From t your town, you continue your struggle. Write to me if you face any problem in doing your duty to your country".

He called his wife and introduced Chandru to her and as well as to others.

The first thing Kasturi Bai asked Chandru whether he had anything to eat on the way from his native place far away from the Ashram

Gandhi openly felt sorry for not asking that first question to a person coming from a very long distance. .

" Sir, Madam, Do not worry. I have not taken any thing for the last three days except tea on the intervening stations. My mind was worried whether I would see the leader. I did not think about food. Also I did not have that much money to buy food. Now, after seeing you and madam, I am not hungry at all. I am so happy and so much strong to go back to Pudukottai and fight with the white animals with my bare hands and then eat at Pudukottai. "

Gandhi quickly got up and took Chandru by hands and then in the open courtyard, made him sit while Kasturi Bai brought food on a mud plate. It was Gandhi who fed Chandru with his hands and it was the turn of Chandru to shed tears. After wiping up the tears, Gandhi asked Chandru to take rest and later he could return back to his native place.

Thus the father of the nation initiated Chandru in to freedom struggle. But where Chandru parted ways, with the national leader, has been taken as the main theme of this book.

MEETING

6

TWO

(In 1939, Gandhiji was in Bombay. (Refer:Mahadev Desai (left) reading out a letter to Gandhi from the viceroy at Birla House, Mumbai, April 7, 1939 –google- search).

Chandru was at Bombay slum at that time. He had changed his name, appearance and had been living in the slum, working as a construction company coolie in the day and making his own plans to avenge the killing of Indians by the foreigners. When he heard that Gandhiji had arrived at the city, he dressed himself neatly with white kurtha and pyjama like the congressmen and went to meet Gandhi at Birla house. There was quite a crowd and he tried to get an audience with the great man but no one was giving listening to him as they were also waiting for their opportunity to see the leader. Patiently Chandru waited throughout the day and evening with out going for food or tea or coffee in the long corridor, while all others were going out and coming back as they wished. Chandru felt that he had no chance of seeing Gandhiji when so many big leaders themselves were waiting for his darshan. But he remained in the same place, eagerly waiting for the big opportunity. It was past ten O clock and still people were going in and coming out with out any let up. Around eleven in the night, the crowd thinned down to a few and still Chandru found no one noticing him waiting from the morning.

At last, there was no one around and suddenly, Chandru sprang to action and tried to rush in big mahogany door. But those who were inside, could be servants, Chandru thought, asked him to come on the next day as Gandhiji had retired to his room. Chandru pleaded that he had been waiting for the darshan of the leader, from the morning. But they did not listen to him but asked him to come again. Chandru said that he would not go back with out seeing the leader even if was physically thrown out. His staccato voice brought a few assistants and leaders who were staying with Gandhiji to the main hall. They also told Chandru to come later as Gandhiji had a tough day and he had more programs on the next day also. They wanted Chandru not to disturb him if he was really interested in the welfare of the leader. Chandru was about to leave the place, when from the upstairs room, Gandhiji came out to see what was the commotion almost at the midnight. When Chandru saw Gandhiji, he forgot everything, he ran over the steps of the staircase three at a time and stood before Gandhi, with folded hands, he asked,

" Sir, do you recognize me- the lion from the caves of south". Gandhiji was looking at Chandru intently for a few seconds. He then smiled and put his hands over his shoulders and took him inside his retiring room where Kasturba was reading a book. Those who were chasing the mad person were pacified by Gandhiji, who told them,

"Hare- Desai bai (to his personal secretary) do not worry about him- he is my little master- he is like you- a great patriot and a lion-hearted person who is waging war against the British single-handedly- you know. Ask others not to make noise-If Pandit (Jawaharlal Nehru) wakes up, he would take me into task for not taking rest" while addressing the chasing crowd of leaders and servants, Gandhiji was hugging Chandru.

"When did you come, my son?" he sat on the white covered quilt.

Chandru after wishing Kasturba who stopped reading and started looking at the new comer.

" Sir, I have been waiting from the morning. I saw big leaders going in and coming out. I requested for an appointment with you. No one listened as they were also waiting to see you, like me. Now fifteen minutes before, when no one was around I tried. They said no and asked me to come tomorrow." Chandru felt that it was enough to start with.

Gandhiji said." Betae, (son- in English) please forgive this old man, for making wait for hours to see me. I am no longer in the politics. I have handed over the charge of the party to Pandit, in 1934 itself. But still, the party functionaries are not satisfied. They want me to take part in the party politics. (In 1934 Gandhi formally resigned from politics, being replaced as leader of the Congress party by Jawaharlal Nehru. Gandhi travelled through India, teaching ahimsa). Ba- do you know who this young lion is? "

He looked at his wife with an expectation. She was known for remembering faces. But she looked bewildered.

8

"Hare Ram! You do not recognize this toofan (cyclone). He came when he was a boy to Sabarmati with out eating for days". Then Kasturba remembered and not only remembered, got up and came and sat by the side of Chandru, stroking his hair, like a true mother.

" Betae, thumne jo kutch kiya- accha nahi kiya(what you have done was not correct). Suppose in the fight with the British, if only you were caught or killed, how your parents would feel or how we would feel. Have you not thought about all those things?" She was looking straight in to his eyes and talked.

Suddenly, she got up again and said,

" Betae, mujae maf karoge (my son, can you forgive me?). Babuji, did you ask him whether he had taken food from the morning when he was waiting here to see you?"

(She asked in Hindi). Gandhiji looked at his wife with a sheepish face and said that he was becoming too old to observe the basic rules of hospitality.

But Chandru understanding what was going on between the husband and wife, intervened and said that he did not want anything to eat, as he was not hungry. But Kasturba disappeared through a rear door, muttering something to her.

Chandru stood up. " Sir, I came to see you. I am happy that I have done what I wanted. But you need rest like those persons interested in your well being said. Hence, I will go and take the food from Ma'am and go to the corridor to eat and take rest till the morning. You and Ma'am take rest after the continuous talking and discussing with so many leaders who came to consult you today   If it is possible for you to spare half an hour to me tomorrow, anytime convenient to you, I will tell you what I have done after I left your Ashram nine years before. Then I will leave you alone, to continue my lonely mission, sir."

On hearing Chandru's self-reproach about his gate crash visit to see him, Gandhiji laughed and said philosophically, " betae, I do not spare time for any one. They spare their time for me to   exchange my views. From morning 4 am, till I find time to rest, I am always ready to meet those who are ready to meet me. So, when you are

9

seeing me now, why do you want to see me tomorrow to tell about your activities for the past nine years? Come on tell me now. Sleep can wait. I control it as I like it and never allow it to control me, till now"

In the meantime, Kasturba brought a plate full of hot rotis and some subji (Hot wheat flour round shaped cake with some side dish).

"Chandru go and eat. In the meantime, I will do the work which I generally complete before my sleep" so saying he took his long notebook and diaries and started his work earnestly.

Kasturba gave the empty plate and made Chandru to sit by her side. She was giving the rotis one by one to him. He was suddenly remembering his mother who, a poor lady, with six children, never had the pleasure of feeding her children like Ma'am. Money and health were the two deciding factors for happiness, he thought. With out knowing how much he had taken, looking at the lady who was more than his mother, Chandru was going on consuming the rotis given to him by Kasturba. Suddenly he felt that he had consumed more than he could. He belched loudly, disturbing Gandhiji at work. He immediately said sorry to him.

He got and washed and thanked Kasturba and kissed her hands for the wonderful dinner, served with love and affection. By then Gandhiji folded his notebook and dairy and was ready to hear what Chandru wanted to say.

He asked his wife to take rest as he was going to hear Chandru giving the details of what had happened in Pudukottai a few years back, when many foreigners, were killed by a guerrilla type attack, creating a national sensation. Kasturba on hearing the subject matter of Chandru's confession quietly came and sat next to Gandhiji on the remaining portion of the white quilt.

When he saw both the husband and wife were ready to hear him, Chandru started his tale of woes or adventures or both.
" Sir and Ma'am, after you got me my return ticket to Pudukottai and some cash for expenses, I reached Pudukottai. I wanted to take rest for a few days, before I embarked on my plan. But the electric effect of seeing you in person and your encouraging and kind words, made me to implement my plan immediately. Before doing that, I

talked to the teacher, the royal coach-driver and the congress activists like me, about my visit to your village and how I was treated by you so nicely etc. On seeing your letter which I did not give it to Madras congress group, they all praised me for meeting and talking with you, personally. They started treating me differently afterwards; they respected me as a member. But I did not disclose my secret plan to any one.

On the next day, I dressed up neatly with the best I had at home and after bidding farewell to my mother, I went straight to the palace of the foreigners, with a bag full of electric repair tools. There I introduced my self as an electrician and tried to get entry into the private quarters of the British officers. When I was stopped by the Indian sentries and Indian officials, I lied and boldly told them that I was asked to come only by the British officer.

Then I was taken to the first floor where I was made to wait. When the British officer saw me, he immediately shouted at me for having bluffed. By then, the sentry who accompanied me started violently pushing me to the entrance. But I surprised him and suddenly broke loose of his grip and rushed to the British officer and shouted at him, using all the English filthy words and some in Tamil also. When he saw me abusing him, profusely, he took a baton from the sentry and started thrashing me, black-and-blue. But I was prepared for the attack and I got hold of the baton and returned the blows with all the strength I could muster. He was trying to defend himself and hence he received most of the blows on his left hand. He was crying and shouting for the armed guards. Within a few minutes, I was overpowered by five guards who took me to the jail inside the palace where I was turned into a human flesh pulp. My hand was broken and I did not know what had happened to me. But later I was told that I was laughing incessantly I was past the stage of remembering anything- I was inwardly happy- I did what I wanted to do from my boyhood.

When I woke up after the third day, I was taken to the court. The Indian judge was listening to the charges against me which ran like a railway line for miles between two stations. But when I was asked to accept the guilt, suddenly a big commotion took place outside the court. All those who were sitting inside the court, went out to see eagerly what caused the commotion outside. Within a few minutes, all the court servants, including the judge were running out.

Unfortunately for the British legal system and fortunately for a hapless Indian criminal like me, the wife of the Viceroy of the Pudukottai Princely state had just collapsed when she was getting into her car. That sensational news had upset all the government activities and brought them to a grinding halt. Unfortunately the guards who brought me to court stood by my side safely handcuffed to me.

After half-an-hour wait, I was whisked to the central jail Pudukottai and there I remained with out any trail for three years. If only the trial was conducted on that fateful day, I would have been dead and gone. But Prudence saved me from the threshold of death. Here I am narrating the incidents today.

One morning, after three years of languishing in the jail, I was asked to meet a magistrate. When he asked me to tell the crime I committed and also the sentence I received. I thought for a fraction of a second. I put on an innocent face and told him that I was also wondering why I was kept in the prison and what crime I had committed. He did not believe. He called for the records and the court assistant came back and delivered a file. But when he went through the contents, he
was looking confused. He again consulted the clerk, who also scratched his head. Then the magistrate announced that I had served the sentence as per records and hence I was free to leave. I thanked the wonderful magistrate and his helpful clerk and walked out, happily. But I did not go home, because I was afraid of the magistrate who might find out the truth and come after me, for putting me behind the bars again. But nothing of that sort happened, as I expected. I came to know later that on the day when the viceroy's wife died, all the government work came to a standstill but it continued for a few more days. In the confusion that followed in all the departments, some how the case papers relating to me got messed up somewhere and my case file was empty with the red tag with out the contents. Fearing reprimand from higher officials our good Indian staff had quietly suppressed the case and when the heat died down, they disposed of my case and buried my file in the old records, forever.

I was free to indulge in my next plan, for which I had already made the groundwork when I was serving the sentence. Immediately after I was lodged in the prison cell, the prison doctors put   the plaster of

Paris bandage over my badly hurt right arm, after placing the broken bones in their normal position. I was with the sling for three months, but the broken bone did not get back to its original shape. Still I have a bent in the right arm. See" Chandru paused to show his arm to Gandhiji. Then satisfied that he had shown his broken arm to the couple, he resumed:

"After two continuous years with in the cell. I was given the first out door duty to sweep the roads in and around the jail. We were three persons entrusted with the job on rotation. Once when I was sweeping the road outside the jail, I noticed a tin sheet covered semicircle shed, some 200 yards from the jail, within the local armed forces campus. There was no compound wall and the place was fully covered with need trees, giving lot of shades everywhere. I noticed some guards with riffles stationed at the back and front of the shed. I wanted to know what they were guarding and what was inside the shed. But I could not ask any one. But one day, I casualty asked the Indian warden whether the shed was a cremation ground for the British officers. He laughed for five minutes and then told me the truth. It was not a cremation shed, but what was inside the shed could cremate thousands of Indians. He added that it was the ammunition godown for the entire Pudukottai state.

From then on, I took personal interest in the godown and casually extended the area of my work. One day, I went to the guards and volunteered to sweep the place clean. They laughed at me, thinking that I had mistaken the shed to be a part of the jail. They did not object to my sweeping the place thereafter. I also told the other two that I would take the tougher outside work from that day onwards. They also laughed at me.

For six months, my hands were sweeping and my eyes and mind were looking for something which might help me to get into the shed with out being observed by the guards. Repeated close observations produced the desired results. The shed on the rear side had a defect not noticed by the guards. Two of the iron nuts on the riveted sheets from inside must have become rusted as I could see some gap at the joint of the sheets at the bottom where they remained embedded with the ground. . It was only my guess, as I had no opportunity to go inside. As I sweeper, I could get a clear picture of the loose sheets, but the sentries always marching up and down with their loaded guns never bothered to check every bold and nut, at least once in years. It opened up new vista for me to avenge for each of blood shed by the Indians in their struggle to drive away the foreigners from our own land.

In the next six months, the Magistrate released me. I decided to act with in the shortest possible time, taking advantage of my contact with the guards at the shed. But I felt that I needed some help from the local radical group and from the congress party members who were all elders and were following your principles to the letter.. I got the information about the radical group only from the jail mates who came to know about my attack on the British officer. I met one Santhanam, an iyengar chap of my age, who also like me, hated the foreigners. We two went to an old farm house surrounded by tress and bushes, at Thirumaiyam a nearby small village, where I was introduced to three more from the group. No one could even imagine that there was a building inside the miniature jungle like thick foliage. The building was as much dilapidated as it was lonely. That was the rendezvous of the radicals. I was given something to eat. We all waited and before evening all other active members reported from the nearby villages and Pudukottai.

I was introduced, but most of them were already knew about me and my abuse and attack on the foreigner. Then I was asked to speak as I only wanted to convene the meeting of the members urgently.

" I am happy to meet like-minded people like you. O.K. Now, I am not going to explain my plan in detail, but I want all of you to do exactly what I want you to do. I will fix the time, day and date. On that happiest day of our life, all of you come with as many persons like you as possible, with whatever weapons you can manage to get, gate crash the palace of Pudukottai and enter the private quarters of the British officers and the Viceroy, to do what every Indian should have done two hundred years back- kill those white invaders mercilessly- but sparing the lives of the ladies and the children. What I would do at that time, would be kept by me as a secret as I do not want my plans to go wrong even by one in a thousand chance, as I am risking all your lives. Do not press for any further details. I may get you weapons and other things, also, required for attacking the British who has the support of the garrison at their peck and call. Understand. It may take three months at the most. But I will keep you posted of the developments in my plan through Santhanam here. O.K. Jai Hind"

Two days after the meeting , I went to see my old friends – the guards of the ammunition shed. On seeing me, they were happy. When they came to know that I was released, they were happier still. I then put on my usual innocent face and begged them to allow me to remain somewhere nearby, cleaning the place, doing some services for them as I could not get any work as an ex-convict in the town. Two of the hoards who had replaced my old friends were not in favour of my presence there near the sensitive area, but the leader happened to know me for the six months.

I was cleaning the place, cooking food for them sometimes, massaging their aching legs, cleaning the riffles, and generally making them comfortable, by sweating out for fifteen hours per day, with sole aim of annihilating the British on our soil.

Just as I expected, I was treated as if I was also a guard like them- a security clearance freely given to me. That was the reward I wanted from those Indian slaves working faithfully for the foreign dogs. I used to sing sometimes which would make them go to sleep with the breeze form the neem trees. On one such occasion, I went to the rear side, where I had seen the riveted nuts were worn out and had come out loose, at the bottom where the sheets were embedded to the ground. I carefully opened the adjoining iron sheets, where the nuts had come out due to rust over years of rain and sun, and tried to get inside. The sheets opened up enough to accommodate me and once I was inside, I was able to keep the sheets back to it original place. Thus I ensured that no one could even imagine that the sheets were tampered with. on the rear side of the shed.

I then came out and started sleeping in my usual place under the neem tree far away from the shed. I waited for the new moon day. That night, I knew that the guards on duty would be my old friends. On some pretext, I went out to the town and came back only after nine in the night. It was pitch dark. I did some work for them and was massaging the legs of the leader while singing the folk songs which I had learnt from my mother, who used it as a lullaby. When the guard who trusted me and the others who trusted their head guard, were dozing with the riffles on their knees, I took out the

15

chloroform which I got from Santhanam, from my underwear, opened the container and placed the same under the nostrils of all the guards for a few seconds. Santhanam warned me that excess of smelling the gas would result in death. I did not want those who trusted me t o die.

After wards, I went to get the cement powder in a bag, which I had hidden near the compound wall. Carrying the bag, I entered the shed through the rear side loose sheets and there I started my work of wrecking the ammunition strength earnestly, lighting the candle I had brought along with the cement bag. I opened the gun powder deal wood boxes and mixed the cement power freely. Then I went out to the well at the far end of the shed and brought water in the big steel bucket. I poured water enough to make the cement mix with the gun powder to make it loose its igniting power. Thus it took two hours for me to make the gun powder stock powerless. I then packed the hand pistols and guns/riffles cartridges in the cement bag, and carried them to the well and there I emptied the contents in the deep well. I did the same for all other types of ammunition- some were like balls –(later I came to know they were hand grenades) I was working non-stop, for five hours from ten thirty in the night to three thirty in the early morning. Now and then , I went to check the guards whether they were still under the influence of the chloroform. I ensured that the shed contained no harmful ammunition in the form of gun powder or any other lethal charges which would kill the Indians

I then went to the compound wall and signalled with a lighted dry branch of a tree. I got the response from the darkness. With in minutes, a few of the members of our group appeared from the darkness. To them , I gave the pistols, cartridges, round balls, riffles, guns, gun powder bag etc. I told them to start the attack exactly at 4 am when I would manage to get in to the palace from the back side. Because, the ammunition shed was on the backside of the palace of course at a safe distance, there were so separate sentries posted for guarding the backside of the palace. That was a blessing in disguise for me. I carried my bag full of my life time ambition in the form of pistols, gun powder and balls, climbed the pipe line and landed on the long corridor, guarded by Indian security men.

I waited patiently. Some where in the distance, the clock tower of Pudukottai chimed four. That was our prearranged signal. Suddenly,

I heard the roaring noises of people from the entrance side of the palace. I knew that my group had commenced the attack. I ignited the gun powder bag and
after breaking the glass panel of the room, I threw it inside and ran towards the front of the building. There was a blinding light and a thunderous sound. The gunpowder had burst open in the room, illuminating the early morning sky. The attack from the front with the weapons I gave to the members, was in full swing when I was throwing the balls after igniting them with the match stick inside the glass panelled rooms after breaking the glasses with the riffle I was carrying. There was commotion and gunfire started from everywhere. My members were all also firing at the guards who returned the fire with the ammunition they had. I told the members to allow the guards to exhaust their supply with them and then only enter the building, which they did.

With in half-an-hour, the whole town woke up and there were hundreds of people gathered   around the palace – more and more were running towards the palace. That was what we wanted and waited for. With in the same half an hour, the palace became a battle ground and a war was waged and won, exactly like how they had won - they came to our country for doing business but settled to rule us by dividing the Indians. I did the same thing and unsettled them- if not all of them- at least those who were in the princely state, Sir. Once I was assured that all the foreigners in the palace, were dead I gave the orders for disbursal quietly as per our plans. While leaving the palace, I saw dead bodies of the British officers and soldiers were strewn here and there. Unfortunately for us, the viceroy who was scheduled to return to Pudukottai, did not make it and was held up at Madurai. So he was the only one to escape from the attack. As per our plans, all of us, except four who were killed in the encounter, escaped in the direction of Vedaranyam, a sea front near Pudukottai. I was past caring about my life. I did my duty to my state and town. I went place to place moving in the night only and resting in some remote abandoned lonely place covered by bushes and trees. For four days, I slogged along, taking water wherever I found and avoid meeting any one-with out food. I knew that there would have been a biggest manhunt by the British Raj and hence, I avoided thinking about food and rest.

Finally, I reached I thought I had reached the tip of the country from where I had planned to go to Ceylon to escape from the British rule.

But where I went was in the opposite direction and I was in the hilly areas of the Travancore Samasthanam. But by then I could get many things to eat like the plantains, wild berries, like Klakka, Ichambazham, coconuts, guava, and even mangoes. But all those fruits items upset my digestive system and I had dysentery for a few days. I did not have money, food and a place to go. I wandered aimlessly only in the hilly areas avoiding the plains, carefully. On the way, the poor tribes living in the hilly areas helped me, with food and some worn out warm clothes. They spoke in a language not known to me, but they recognised my hunger, lack of warm clothing-homeless state, the trade marks of the poor. After four months, I stumbled upon the highway to Bombay. When I reached here, I was looking worse than a beggar with the rags on and a thick dust covered stinking beard, emaciated to the extent of hanging me on a nail in the wall, like a skeleton.

I wandered around in this big city of rich merchants, and finally landed in the Daravi slum areas where I found many Tamilians like me have settled down there for years. They told me that they came with lot of dreams, but they all ended up in the slums, again dreaming of going back to their native places, with money. Sir, I have changed my facial appearance and deliberately created a long scar on the forehead with my knife. I suffered with the wound for two months and then only it healed. Sir, you have recognised me but Ma'am could not easily."

Chandru at last ended his confession-cum- the story of adventures. Gandhiji did not react immediately. The time was thirty minutes past twelve in the midnight. Kasturba had not recovered from the shock of the narratives. She was just sitting but looking blank.

Suddenly, Gandhiji adjusted his posture and sat erect. He looked at Chandru, and said flatly,

" Chandru, though you have done your duty to the nation, yet, please forgive me, if I say, I do not approve of your attack on the sleeping foreigners and killing them en-masse. Agreed, you have your way of showing patriotism, but did it mean that you should follow the same British method of –eye for eye and a tooth for tooth. Subhash Bose, the great patriot insisted on the retaliatory method which I strongly opposed. Why? Let me explain. Chandru and people like you, you should first understand more about the strength of the enemies than having blind faith in your strength, before initiating actions or retaliating an action. If they kill one hundred Indians, they need not sacrifice the life of a single British officer or a soldier, if they want. All they would do is , to order the Indian soldiers to kill the Indians. In that way, they have nothing to lose. Am I correct? Let us look at from another angle- If they kill one hundred Indians, to revenge the killing of one hundred British, how many Indians are required to accomplish the task? You tell me, Chandru, the Lion from the South Indian caves. Come on. In your case, you have killed thirty seven foreigners in Pudukottai- do you know how many innocent Indians were butchered on that day, who were mere spectators of the midnight war? How many women have become widows? Are they war widows? Are they going to get some financial help from you or from the government? Who will look after them and their like after the thoughtless and hasty actions ? Do you think that I am incapable of taking such boorish barbarian action ? No , I can, with millions of people supporting me, ready to sacrifice their life. But why have I not acted like you, do you know, I am accepted as the leader of all those who want freedom to the country. My aim is to get the freedom but with the least cost. Of course, I can also go to war with the British- we can out number them. They may kill more Indians with their modern weapons and we may finally drive them out –but only after sacrificing millions of lives.

Just for picking up a handful of salt from our own sea shore, they had arrested 60000 Indians and what would they not do if I started using violence from the beginning? Think Chandru. Neither I would be alive nor the congress party nor the struggle for independence. How long do you think people would fight till they die against the British? One year, two years or more. Nothing would happened to the invaders- they would make Indians fight between themselves for ever, one as loyal British soldiers and another patriotic Indians. Those who wanted freedom for their country, would not live to enjoy the freedom. Is it fair? If there is a way with which we can achieve the end result with out much expense, should we not as prudent persons choose the trouble-free or cost-less path? Now you must understand, my young man, what you have done was, like pricking a sleeping lion with a penknife on its thick upper skin and running away before it woke up to show its strength. So, I Gandhi, one of the Indians participating in this struggle for independence to the country, demand a promise from you, that you give up your bloodthirsty approach to removing the foreigners from out soil, from his moment-" Gandhiji was extending his right hand expecting the hand of Chandru to clasp it as a token of making the promise. But Chandru was sitting like a stone idol. His mouth was half open and his eyes stood still. Gandhiji had to shake him violently to activate his senses.

Chandru woke up from the trance and looked sheepishly at the leader. He saw the extended hand of the leader and then looked up to see Gandhiji. He was repeating that action more than two times, when Gandhiji signalled him to promise. He did what he was asked, but, while doing so, he added,

" Sir you are really great . That is why people from all over the country come to you for advice. But I am Chandru- a simple person. For me, freedom means –driving away the foreigners in my place. because I am not leader like you. I am not bound to achieve any promise, because I have not made any promise. Hence, an uneducated person like me, having love for my country, I did what I felt was correct for me and my nation. I had never made any deep analysis like you. I agree with what ever you say I also accept that my hasty action had ruined the lives of innocent people of my town. But, I did not know any other way. From my boyhood, I was stuck with one thought. I should remove the white-men from my place and in their place, I should sit and remove the problems of the people, by remaining as Chandru only and not like the MahaRajas of Pudukottai- staying in big palaces and having hundreds of servants enjoying life at the cost of others, with out doing any work to earn the right of living on the earth. But, if you say, I acted foolishly in giving vent to my individual feelings against the British, I accept my crime. Sir, you are the judge to pronounce the punishment to me, for what I have done to my own people. "

Chandru stood up with a folded hands, as if he was a prisoner waiting for the judgement. Gandhiji laughed aloud on seeing the righteous young patriot seeking punishment courageously owning the responsibility of the mistake he had committed. He also stood up and again asked Chandru to promise him that he would give up violence from that very moment and he ended up by saying that the promise should be considered as a punishment for the acts of violence. Chandru said nothing and placed his palm over the palm of the Apostle of peace and said loudly that he would never again hurt anyone as long as he lived.   But he asked Gandhiji what else he could do if he gave up the only purpose of his existence.

The time was half past one and Gandhiji made a big yawning and declared that it was time for all the three to sleep. He added that he had to wake up at 4 am for his morning walk. He was telling himself that he had lot of work to do on the next day.

Chandru excused himself and was about to leave the room. But Gandhiji asked to sleep in the available place.

Kasturba suddenly spoke as if she was still in the grip of the discussions between Chandru and her husband. " Babuji, (she liked to use the word 'Babuji' whenever they were alone) I am sorry to interfere in the talks between you two. After making his promise, Chandru was asking you what he would do hereafter now that, he would follow your principles of non-violence. You have not told him anything. Can I make a suggestion, Babuji ?" Gandhiji again said sorry to his wife, for a second time that night and asked her to go ahead.

 Kasturba came near Chandru and placing her hands over his shoulder, he asked Chandru,

"betae, . you told Babuji that you wanted to sit in the place of the British or the Indian Kings, to remove the problems of the people. Now, I have seen ever since we came from South Africa, over these years, all of us are only thinking about the ways and means of getting the freedom and I am sure that we have not yet prepared the plans for taking over from the British rule and also we are yet to formulate the norms for governing the free India, to make every one enjoy equally the freedom from day one after Independence. I know many laws were enacted by the British for giving certain rights to the Indians represented by the congress party. But we are yet to prepare the rules and regulations of the new India, with which we should be able to remove all the problems of the poor people all over the land, particularly those from the villages.

I want you, Chandru to devote your time from now onwards to prepare the guidelines for administrating the Independent India, removing all the disparities between the Harijans and the non-Harijans, rich and the poor, urban and the village, educated and

21

the uneducated, Hindu and Muslims, South and North, and finally between men and women. That is the Ram Rajya, Babuji has been dreaming over all these years. You take up the task, Oh the Lion from the Southern caves. I am confident- you will accomplish the work you take. Good luck, my son", she shook hands with Chandru, while Gandhiji clapped his hands for a long time.

"Ba(Kasturi was called 'Ba' by her husband), aaj mei bahuth kush hoom. (I am very happy today). I know you are a keen observer and had been a good advisor whenever I was facing some tricky situations in the past. But today, you have excelled all your past records" he turned towards Chandru and said ,

"you have a job to do. From now start doing it. I know You can read and write English well. But you should take one more work- seriously. Learn to read, write and speak fluently Hindi- the common language for binding all the Indians. Go and collect the materials from the Library and if you want any help, meet me at any time. But concentrate on these important assignments which we have not yet taken up as it is felt by the party that the time has not come for drafting the constitution of the new India.

What Kasturi was telling you about the rules and regulations , refer to New Indian Constitution. We have with us very many lawyers like Ambedkher and other senior lawyers who can do the job well. But as Kasturi said, I also want the new constitution to be written by an ordinary person who wants the freedom should be enjoyed by every one of the Indians irrespective of many differences subsist between them in the society, even if such person is not from the legal fraternity. I want a man with a lot of common sense and human kindness to draft the new constitution- that person should have personal experience of poverty, should know first hand, the struggles of existence at the village level and top of it, he should be honest and patriotic. Chandru, you are my man- keep it as a secret and I know you are the fittest person for the job given to you. Good luck and now , really we should sleep at least for two hours."
With in a few minutes, Gandhiji and Kasturba were fast asleep. Chandru sat there quietly was looking at them in the dim light coming from the over hanging electric night lamp. Suddenly he got up and took out a pencil from the pen stand where there were many pens and pencils, ready for use. He searched for a plain sheet of paper , but found nothing except the long note book and

the diary of Gandhiji, besides books. He then looked around and saw a calendar hanging from the wall. It was with his easy reach. He quietly removed a sheet belonging to an earlier month - February 1939, and there on the backside wrote legibly taking efforts to control his handwriting.

Most Respected Sir,

I am leaving right now- to start the work you and ma'am have given. Don't mistake me for leaving the place with out taking your permission. I am already a criminal wanted for a very big crime by the British Rulers. But if I am seen with you, the focus of attention might fall on me too and that would make the British to probe. If by any chance, they find out who I am, I do not care what they do with me. But just because I am found with you, I do not want you to suffer on my account. I have already killed several innocent Indians with out knowing what I was doing. But I can never even dream of harming you, even by a remotest chance. Thank you for giving a new meaning to my life. I will do what I have been asked to do. I will me you after I accomplishing the task entrusted to me. Jai Hind. Chandru-a harmless lion. " He placed the calendar sheet carefully on the diary and placed a paper weight over it. Then he lied down but was wide awake- trying to think about what Gandhiji told about him. Somewhere in the house the grandfather's clock chimed . It was 3 O'clock in the morning.

Chandru did not wait for the noble couple to wake up. He got up quietly after the two had slept. He went to the corridor and there he was lying down for the day to dawn. He knew that Gandhiji would wake up for the morning walk. But around three thirty in the morning, he left the Birla House and once outside, the April sea breeze gave a refreshing and soothing feeling to Chandru, who was walking briskly towards his hut in the Daravi slum. After many years, he had taken stomach full of food which gave him trouble, against which the lion from the southern cave, could not fight.

MEETING THREE

QUITIN1   QUITIN2.   QUITIN7.

QUITIN5.

Acknowledgement:

"http://commons.wikimedia.org/wiki/Category:Quit_India_Movement
"

Browse categories: History of India

On 8th August 1942, Gandhiji announced the 'Quit India movement ' throughout the country. Every where the leaders were arrested and jailed. Gandhiji was arrested on 9th August 1942 and imprisoned in the Aga Khan palace Pune. The British government had ruthlessly suppressed the struggle by killing many patriots with out a trial. Indian National Congress was declared an illegal institution

On reading the news that Gandhiji was arrested with Kasturba and kept in Aga Khan Palace Pune, Chandru who was at that time, roaming in the villages in Andhra Pradesh, immediately took the train to Pune and there, he waited patiently outside the palace unmindful of the night weather conditions in the hilly areas. On the third day, a group of persons, looking like press reporters were allowed to see Gandhiji in the palace. Chandru had brought with him a set of white kurtha and pyjama. Wearing them, he also joined the group, having permission to see the prisoner.

On a spacious room, but guarded by sentries with guns, the great leader was sitting with his usual charka and was spinning the yarns effortlessly. All those who came to see him, paid their respects to him. They were then chatting with him in Hindi, watched like a hawk by the English officer standing very close to the prisoner. Suddenly,

Gandhiji had spotted Chandru whom he knew was not belonging to the group. On meeting eye to eye with Gandhiji, Chandru moved little closer to the leader.

Chandru tried to talk in a low volume, worried about the British officer observing everything that was going on. Gandhiji did not react immediately, smiled. He then turned his attention to the group and the officer had announced that the time for meeting was over. Chandru was choking with sadness- after taking so much efforts to meet the leader to tell him, what he had done during the past three years, he was disappointed to see the antic-climax.- Gandhiji had not even recognized him. Chandru was ready to leave with others when suddenly Gandhi stopped his charka and came along with the crowd to see them off at the door of the hall.

When Gandhiji was moving side by side with Chandru very closely he whispered, "young lion, Do not worry that I have not talked to you. Go and meet Ba. After my release meet me. God bless you". He smiled and waved at the group, which included Chandru, who was in cloud nine- but suppressed his overflowing emotions with great difficulty.

He then accompanied the same group to see Kasturba who was kept separately in another room.

After paying their respects to the mother of the nation, the members of the group were talking to her. But an Indian sentry /guard was away standing near the entrance- some 10 metres away from her. Chandru felt that it was 'now or never' opportunity. He quickly moved side ways to reach with in a metre of where the lady was sitting. On seeing Chandru in the group, Kasturba was surprised. But she did not reveal herself. But casually smiled at Chandru and asked him whether he was doing his work satisfactorily. Chandru wanted to tell everything but the meeting with her was restricted to minutes. Hence he simple said that he had covered all the villages in many provinces and still it might take a few years to complete the job given to him. She then started talking to the group. The time for leaving was announced by the guard and Chandru touched the feet of the great lady as a mark of his love and affection for her, and left with the group silently.

Once outside the palace complex, Chandru quietly retreated to a lonely spot where he cried and cried, with happiness till he felt enough. " young lion- meet Ba. Meet me after my release" he was muttering those words again and again- he was telling himself, " who said all those words- the great Gandhiji- the fighter and destroyer of the foreigners" . He was happy and suddenly he became very hungry. But in that place, there was not even a petty shop leave alone a dhaba or eating joint

MEETING FOUR

1944- Feb 22 Kasturba died in detention at Aga khan palace at the age of seventy-four

On hearing the news, Chandru who was in a village near Ernakulam , rushed to Pune like a mad man, suppressing his sorrows to the extent possible. The fellow-travellers in the train were surprised when they came to know the reason for the non-stop crying of the English speaking beggar. By the time he reached Pune, her godmother had been cremated. When he realised that he would not be able to see her mortal remains thereafter for ever, he lost control himself and was crying aloud like a child, creating a scene. The guards and others who had come to pay their homage to Gandhiji standing in the queue tried to pacify him. But he fainted partly due to the shock of the death of Kasturba and partly due to his physical weakness, after three days travel with out food and sleep, grieving all the time.

When he woke up, he was on a knitted jute cot at the corner of a big room. He did not where he was. When he tried to get up, he was feeling giddy. He was not well. His head ached and his body was hot. He could not call any one. Words did not come out. Fortunately, some one passed the corridor and on seeing Chandru trying to get up, the white-clad lady in her late fifties, smiled and asked him to take rest, as he was having high fever.

On the second day, when he woke, he was felling better. He remembered vaguely about taking medicines and some hot liquid food he did know- when.

When he got up and tried to stand, he realised his weakness-caused by the fever. But somehow, he managed to leave the room, but he was stopped by a guard who asked him to get back to his room. Chandru folded his shaky hands and begged that guard to permit him to see Gandhiji. On seeing the pitiable conditions of the Indian beggar, he asked Chandru to go right and after a few yards, he would find the Gandhi's room.

When Chandru managed to reach the room where Gandhiji was kept, he saw good many persons, silently, sitting before Gandhiji, all appearing to be leaders from the Congress parties, besides a few foreigners and three or four Indian women of assorted age. When Gandhiji saw Chandru, he smiled and called him to his side. But Chandru again lost his control and started crying , uncontrollably. Two visitors had to help Chandru to make him sit near Gandhiji. Chandru fell on his feet and continued his crying. Gandhiji stroked his messy hair, patted his back affectionately and bent forward to whisper, " Betae, you are a lion. Your mother has completed her work and has gone. I will also go once I feel that I have done my work. What happened to the work entrusted to you by your mother? Have you done it?"

On hearing Gandhiji talking about the work entrusted to him, Chandru recovered to some extent from his overflowing emotional outburst and got up to say "Yes Sir".

Gandhiji immediately, introduced Chandru to those who were present-

" Pandit, Patel, friends, please meet the lion from the southern dark caves. He is- sorry- he was an one man army. What he did, I cannot tell you now. But he has become my adopted son. He has given up his life time ambition and started becoming an ambassador of non-violence. Ba had given him a work. He says that he has completed. But again I cannot discuss about it now. But hereafter he should be with me only because, I do not want him to get another shock of not seeing my body when I die. Chandru, you should stop those tear drops. They should be only for those poor Indians who are suffering in villages with out food, clothes and shelter. Do you understand. Now go and get ready to join us for the prayer."

He gave a small pat on his head and turned his attention to the leaders who were looking shocked on hearing Gandhiji calling some one as his adopted son. But Patel and Pandit Nehru knew the background history of the beggar like Chandru.

MILESTONE
TWO
IN POLITICS

From 25 February 1944 till he was foolishly shot dead by a Hindu fanatic on 30th January 1948, Chandru was one of the few who had remained with him as his shadows. On the night of his first day stay with him at the Aga Khan palace, permitted specially by the English officer who was a witness to the scene created by Chandru in front of the palace court yard, Chandru remained with Gandhiji in his same room. When he was trying to help, Gandhiji flatly refused to take help from him. He said that he was not bedridden and sick.

He then told Chandru very clearly the terms of his permanent stay with him-

"Betae, one thing you should remember. You are not that person you think you are - now I am not that person you think I am. Do you understand the meaning? Chandru- have you seen the faces of those people here in the afternoon, today when I said that you were my adopted son? I know- you have missed, but I have not. All along those leaders from different parts of the country have done so much in continuing the struggle sacrificing their family life, wealth, their lucrative profession, their peace of mind and above all, ready to lay their life in the process. I am close to them and they have regards for me, But, today, I introduced you, a rank outsider or a stranger to those who have been in the political field for decades.   Naturally, they would like to know who you were and how you could come so close to me? Etc. Only Patel and Pandit knew about you. But the two of them already were too eager to meet you. Only I have prevented them from bringing you to the open forum fearing recognition by the British.

Now Chandru you should follow my advice. As long as you are with me, which you must, you should keep your ears open and eyes and mouth shut. You know why- Ba wanted to see you before she died. She told me to take care of you. She was so much attached to you. That is why, when I see you- I feel like seeing Ba in you. It was her last wish- I was there- my sons were all there- many other were there- looking at her losing her grip over her earthly life-then suddenly she asked " Chandru is there". I said close to her ears. "No- he may not be aware of your sickness. I will bring him if you promise to live till he comes". But there was a semblance of a wry smile- I thought- it was not –but she took time to say " take care of the li....on". Thereafter I did not hear her talking for three hours till she became permanently silent."

On seeing Chandru was crying holding the fragile hands of his master, Gandhiji lifted his face and asked him to stop crying as he did not his Ba in him to shed tears. Those words worked wonders for Chandru- he immediately stopped crying and looked at Gandhiji as if to ask him to continue his advice.

" So Chandru- be with me, wherever I go. But remain at a distance not far away. But never show your closeness to me, in the presence of others, like Ba. But when we are alone, tell me your candid views on the talks I had with the visitors, leaders, press reporters and others. Ba did the same thing. I want you to be highly critical of my decisions, my advice to others, and my speech etc. But only when we are alone. Even if you have your own views which might be contradicting mine, do not worry. I promise you- I will never get angry with you, even if you are right and I am proved wrong not once – more than once-.Be my alter ego. Be my Ba" he paused for a few seconds and continued- Chandru could see a noticeable change in his voice when he talked about his life partner for more than fifty years.

" Today I have neither my Ba nor my Mahadev Desai, my secretary who left in a hurry when was just 42. He died of a heart attack I could not believe. Here I am at 74- still living- but a 42 year old young man died because I accept, I must have consumed all his energy given to him by the god, sufficient for one hundred years, during the time when he was working with me as my key man".

Thereafter, he asked Chandru to take rest as he had to complete the work which he should do everyday before going to bed.

PRIVATE DISCUSSIONS WITH GANDHIJI

ONE

It was the first opportunity Chandru got to discuss with his mentor freely. Gandhiji was in still in the Aga Palace. It was He was not well for the past few days and was given medicines and doctors came and checked him often. All the appointments and visitors were cancelled and stopped, except Patel and Pandit. Gandhiji though weak was restless and was trying to get back to active life, but his health did not permit him.

Chandru was at his bedside, simply looking at him and not sleeping. When Gandhiji woke up suddenly he saw Chandru sitting close to his bed and was wide awake. He chided him for not sleeping and also for remaining too close to him as he might also contract the same fever. But Chandru smiled and held his soft hands and smoothly pressed them while requesting to him to sleep.

Then Gandhiji told him that he was almost normal and he never feel like sleeping any more- as he had slept enough during the past three days. He wanted Chandru to tell him what he wanted to tell him- though he would listen, he would not reply. It was forty minutes past eleven in the night. Chandru begged him to sleep as it was not the time to ask questions or express one's views to a sick person.

When Gandhiji asked him whether he was ready to disobey his orders, Chandru, with many apologies told him what he was having in his minds for years:

" India as only a few know, was not one nation having one language, one caste, one religion etc. Its political map was changed from time to time, and those who ruled her, either as small kings in every corner of the land or as Emperors, they had never attempted to have classless society or remove poverty or remove disparity between rich and poor, or tried to educate every one, or to give free medical aim for all. All sorts, varieties or tiers of people, bearing their perennial problems of existence from birth to death, were living in the kingdoms whether ruled by foreign invaders like Muslims or Hindu kings. The high class citizens, privileged

33

courtesans, the relatives and kith and kin of these special class of people, enjoyed life and led a life of pomp and show along with MahaRajahs or Emperors, who decided the fate of his or her subjects. Everything depended on the character, mindset, mood, analytical abilities, educational background, experience, knowledge and the application of them, his or her interest in the development or the welfare of his people etc etc. Hence, one man or woman acting alone or in consultation with a group, determined the life of the majority of the people. This was the famous culture and heritage of the ancient world everywhere. Am I correct ,sir?"

Gandhiji reminded him that he should not ask any questions. Again with another batch of apologies, Chandru resumed his talk:

"In the case of the India, the special culture and heritage were fragmentation of land and kingdoms, people mentally divided on the basis of language, religion, castes, north and south conscience which enabled the invaders to enter the sub continent easily and establish their empire. We know that the Indian history is replete with many evidences of how the disunity among the Northern Kings paved the way for the successful invasions of the Muslims which resulted in their rule in Hindu land for five centuries and how the traders from Great Britain taking advantage of the rivalries among the kings entered the country from the western coast and eventually exploited the country's resources for one hundred and fifty years till now.

My questions are-

Why those who ruled the country before the British empire had not eradicated the poverty of the majority of the people, ensured medical facilities, and provided education for all?
Why were not the people worried about their individual rights during those periods ?
Our history has recorded the existence of many great poets and scholars decorating the courts of the Kings and Emperors in those days and why those intelligent persons always reported in their master pieces, that people were happy, contended and leading a peaceful life?
Where was the spirit of independence in the minds of the people during the Mughal empire who were also foreigners like British ?

What were the points of difference between the Moguls and the British rules, which prompted the Indians to start the struggle for Independence?

Was it because that the British united Indian provinces under one banner from Himalayas to Kanyakumari , from Assam to Gujarat and brought all the Indians together in their struggle for freedom ?

If so, in the days of Asoka, and Aurangaseb also, the Indian sub continent was almost under one rule and why in those periods, the Indians never thought about the Independence?

Is there any recorded historical evidences to show that people in the villages were harassed or killed or troubled or deprived or inconvenienced by the British during their one hundred fifty years of rule?

Whether during the time when the Mogul or the British or the Hindu kings ruled the country , the situation prevailing in the small villages of the sub continent were in the same state not affected by the good or bad rulers ?

Whether the villagers were living with what they had, learning to live within their means and lead a life of mental comfort, enjoying peaceful life irrespective of their religion, castes, wealth, status, with in the boundaries set by themselves, enforced with fairness by the self-nominated village administrators?

Whether they faced drought and flood, epidemic and good harvest with the same equanimity, because they strongly believed that nothing could change their fate and nobody from the high places would come to fight for them.

I would like to know whether any agency had conducted 'on the spot' survey of the conditions prevailing in the villages in those days and whether any one took the trouble of gathering the individual opinions of the villagers?

What was freedom to those traditionally contended people, only in the eyes of a foreigner or affluent or rich city dwellers, a poor lot with a very   low standard of living?

 How many of those unfortunate knew or wanted to know what was freedom to the country when their own freedom from their own perennial problems of day today life was not possible for them to get over for centuries ?

How many of these millions who formed the majority of the population of the country till now, Sir,   knew where was Delhi, who was a viceroy and why the country should have freedom , why it should be ruled by Indians and what was wrong with the British ?

Even now, when I interviewed at least 100000 old people who lived in villages, small towns, cities etc, for the past five years, after my mother had entrusted me the work to prepare the guidelines of administration for the new India, their majority opinion was that they lived with respect, dignity and peacefully with out any of the problems faced by them. That is not the opinion but this happens to be the fact.

Even during the entire freedom struggle, from 1858 in the Union of India, how many millions of poor people at the villages participated actively, forgetting their own day today problems of existence ?

Was there a demand for freedom from these so called impoverished, unhealthy and illiterate people?

Except a few educated and affluent born in this land who could not tolerate the rule of foreigners, (influenced by a utopian idea of democracy, a concept which was getting mass appeal during the time because of the successful American war of Independence), the villagers who formed the statistical majority never bothered or worried about who ruled or what happened to the country. Can you deny my statement sir?

It was because they remained as they were with out any change in their routine life of shortages of every essential things. Unhealthy surroundings, perennial health problems. Borrowings from the shylock-like money lenders and mismatching remuneration given for hard labour for unlimited hours of services by the bloodsucking landlords were some of the commonly treated life hazards for the poor Indians which they had accepted as inevitable curses on them for the sins they might have committed in their previous births. To that extent they were brain washed by the religious leaders enjoying all the comforts and patronage by the rich and the ruling families.

Hence Indians over hundreds of generations had to put up with inconveniences and problems of all sorts in day today life , became immune. Even when they were treated as cattle, sometimes worse than the animals like horses, dogs, and milch animals by their masters, they developed the rare super- human qualities like love for their children, respect for the neighbourhood, gratitude towards the masters, and to top it all, they managed to sleep peacefully with out a worry for the next day, even though they never managed to get what they wanted, that is, the basic needs like food shelter and clothes for the dog's work they did for years till their death. Please accept the fact.. That was the only factor which held them as humans – **their contentment in life with very little facilities and** amenities was the hall mark of the existence of all the millions of majority of the population of this land for thousands of years. If any one in `1944 wants to boast of the culture and heritage of this country, please quote this – under all adverse circumstances of difficult and problematic life, ignoring the ill-treatment of the rich and affluent land lords and the rulers, the majority of our ancestors living in villages never grumbled and raised against for the sake of demanding their rights in the society, and lived peacefully, harmoniously loving each other, forgetting the religion and caste barriers, sharing what they had and sleeping without the fear of the morrows"

Gandhiji, with a his usual mesmerising broad smile, clapped with difficulty. He was shedding tears.

On seeing him crying Chandru stopped. But he was asked to continue.

" The same situation might prevail in majority of the villages in the independent India also. That is my only worry unless we prepare a master plan to include every Indian's personal welfare in the day to day administration of the government of the New India.

Sir, please note,,,if and if only, anytime during any time in the past thousands of years, the villagers' peaceful life was threatened, or if they were made to forego sleep by any issue created by their masters, I am 100% sure that would have collectively revolted not like the cowardly selfish half hearted attempts made by the educated persons of the urban lands. They would have destroyed the intruders and would not have slept till they were assured of their right to have a contended simple life and a peaceful sleep. Fortunately, for the Kings and the Emperors or Moguls or British, they ignored them, forgot them; none meddled with them and their unenviable life and left them to rot as nonentities like the flies and the mosquitoes that enveloped the villages of the Indian subcontinent, sharing their existence with the godforsaken human species.

Thus, no force of any physical magnitude could have shaken their mindset developed over centuries of accepting what was offered, but for the Thomas Alva Edison's invention of Cinema which is creating havoc in the minds of the Indians demolishing and destroying their mindset for the first time in the history. What the ill-treatment by the rulers over centuries could not do, what the lack of good food, medical facilities and dearth pf wealth and income could not do, what the leaders born now and then among them demanding self respect could not do to awaken them to fight for their legitimate rights, the cinema has started doing now. It was because, the villagers who have been all along meekly seeing their master's family members enjoying life did not attach any meaning for them; they were treating the events as a part of the duties and they knew that they could not even imagine in their life time to get such opportunities . They used to treat such lavish and luxurious life just like the bank cashier treats the public money passing through his hands. But the new medium called cinema where the common man was projected to be enjoying life like the rich landlords and the stories of Gods bestowing boons to the devotees etc are changing the mindset of the villagers slowly and in future I can categorically assert that whatever be the level of general knowledge of the illiterate villagers, they are going to be aware of the cinemas, the heroes, the heroines, the sequences, the dialogues, and more than any thing else the perennial flow of songs.

The reason for the instant success of the cinemas in the midst of the villagers was the stimulus it gave for dreaming themselves enjoying what luxuries had to offer to humans in reality some day in the future before they died. Hitherto they considered luxury as some thing which they could never attain during their life time and thus they had no worries or ambitious plans or yearnings, which enabled them to sleep peacefully. But the cinema is demolishing the peace and sleep . It appears to make them think. It makes them to feel that they too can live luxuriously like the rich. Thus the villagers I am sorry to say sir, after my extensive tour , have started their day-dreaming and thereby loosing the sleep and are gradually beginning to worry about the morrows.

Under these circumstances, what were the reasons for taking up the struggle for Independence only against the British and not against the kingdoms ruled the country earlier?
How the demand for nationalism suddenly sprang up in the minds of the few people after 1858 ?

Independence or freedom was only a perception of the educated middle class developed by only British, who introduced Western education in India by opening colleges/Universities   in the Presidency towns of Bombay, Calcutta and Madras . The aristocratic elite who wanted to take over the power to rule the country from the foreigners, the Banias or the landlords who wanted to start or expand their business without the restriction from the British govt , the communist minded people who wanted to bring changes with the utopian ideas of making the working class to rule their land and finally the perverted and selfish persons brain washing the poor people all joined the struggle for freedom with their individual selfish objectives and ulterior motives. Am I wrong, Sir, in my perception ?

The reason for the soldier's mutiny in 1858, persisted even when the Moguls ruled the country, but were there resentments from the soldiers who were forced to go against their religious faith while performing their duty during their time?

But how could the expression of resentment n religious sentiments could be construed as a fight for   independence from the British Empire ?

Was it not the interpretation of the educated class, who projected the mutiny as the beginning of the war of independence against the British?

The few educated persons under the leadership of a foreigner founded the Congress party in 1885. Had they conducted any survey of the entire country to find out what exactly was going on in the minds of the people of the   country and how people from the villages to the city and from the South to the North and from the east to the West felt about the then prevailing conditions, before staring the Congress party?

If not, at least after the formation had they tried to find out the state of affairs prevailing in the nook and corner of the country?

The founder-members of the party when they started canvassing the support of the like minded people to join the organised struggle in driving away the foreigners   had they attempted to involve the majority of unhealthy, illiterate and impoverished people struggling in the villages from the beginning? If not , why?

That means, why   did not the Congress founded by the middle class, with the objective of getting freedom,   for removing the problems of the people of India,   consider   ensuring the representation of the majority in the party, if not from the beginning, at least some time after its formation?

Why they did not do it till Ambedkher started demanding independent land for the poor and illiterate Harijans ?

Why did you, sir, - announced the fast unto death, protest, to abort the efforts of Ambedkher, with out ensuring adequate representation for the poor in the formation of Indian Government?

How many Congress leaders had been to all or a majority of the villages in the state to which they belonged or at least stayed over nights in villages in their individual capacities with out the pomp and show of a leader, accompanied by a troupe of followers, members of the party etc or lived and suffered in the Indian villages?

Was there any attempt made to make a study or census or survey of the villages, particularly with reference to

the impact on their day today life by their financial and social problems, their views,

their demands,

their opinion about the freedom struggle,

their willingness to participate in the struggle,

their immediate needs , what they expected from the independent country, their idea of religious harmony,

inter-caste issues,

how they liked the abolition of unequal treatment of a section of human beings branding them as Sudhras or untouchales or Harijans or dalits at any time till now or even is there a proposal to take this most important task at least in future before the foreigners give us independence?

When there is so much homework is pending, what is the hurry in getting the power from the British ?

Chandru stopped talking and it was five minutes to two in the early morning. Gandhiji was looking worried and serious. He did not talk to Chandru, but, lied down flat on his cot and simply looked at the ceiling. If only his wife was there, she could have told others that her husband was in deep thoughts. Chandru also did not sleep, but was looking only at Gandhiji. Both of them did not know when they slept.

PRIVATE DISCUSSIONS
WITH GANDHIJI
-2-

Gandhiji asked Chandru to speak out. The time was past midnight. The whole day was spent by Gandhiji with the visitors and some press persons from foreign magazines. Their interviews lasted for a few hours. Instead of retiring to bed, Gandhiji asked Chandru to unfold his thoughts and personal opinions on the Indian struggle for freedom. Till that date, Gandhiji did not even once referred to Chandru about the views expressed by him. But he was asking for a second round of his views with in a month.

Chandru was having enough material to deliver, for what they were worth. He began:

" What I am going to tell you was what I heard from the educated people from different parts of the country, during my travel for the five year. At the Lahore session, in 1929, Sardar Patel who was reported to be close to you, than Pandit Nehru, despite having big support in the CWC, lost his chances of becoming the congress president because of you sir. They said that you had supported, despite the fact, Patel was a man of action unlike Nehru who was a man of dreams and thoughts. The openly alleged that you were enamoured of Jawaharlal's western gloss, who was a Harrow-Cambridge graduate, besides a Barrister and above all, the son of the richest person. They added that you have unknowingly developed an inferiority complex in you and that could be the reason, they all opined that you had selected Nehru as the right man to negotiate with Englishmen. But they also praised you for admonishing Panditji for assuming power in declaring socialism as the government policy of the New India in 1936, itself even before forming the government

Another common criticisms made by many well educated politically knowledgeable persons whom I had met, were about the national and regional level leaders. They were all openly showing their preference to the British or the Soviet policies, with out trying to find out what type of government the country like India suffering for five thousand years and more under various types of government with different sets of rulers, might need. Top of all the leaders, many had expressed shock about Panditji's promise to redraw the political map of the New India on the basis of linguistic uniformities.

The third criticism, I happened to hear, though, only from a few but from many places of the country, was about you, Sir.

The congress became a national party having spread all over the country by your untiring efforts and it was only you, they said , who, for the first time, went to meet the villagers after the formation of the Congress. But, sir, you went everywhere with your usual group of followers. They said, you are a national leader having an image, name and charisma, even though was the only leader to go to people at remote places yet, you did not experience the real problems of the villagers because you never lived in an Indian remote village and led a village life like any other ordinary citizen. You were and are always a visitor and a guest of honour. Hence your perception of the problems of the villagers to that extent have to be unrealistic and lacking personal experience.. Had you gone to stay in a Harijan villages immediately after your return from South Africa with out being a 'somebody' in the Congress or freedom struggle, you could have realised or experienced the actual life of the miserable poor unhealthy and illiterate Indians, much better and your approach would be more realistic and not heresy."

Chandru stopped and looked at Gandhiji to know how he was taking the open criticism of his political activities. He found no change, but he appeared to be perturbed if the parallel lines, formed on his forehead could be taken as indicators of congestion in the human mind.

But on seeing Chandru stopping his talking, suddenly, Gandhiji asked him whether he was feeling tired of telling the truths. Chandru nodded his head horizontally to indicate that he was not. Then he asked him to go ahead and complete the days' quota, fully.

Chandru started with a hesitation :

"If we analyse the overview of the freedom struggle, until now, we find that at no point of time, we have found the dearth of leaders because they were not the first ones to die in any confrontation with the British or Muslim or Hindu and all the struggles were at the cost of lower middle level patriots or grass root level party members or innocent public. No senior leader has been killed either by Muslim or by Hindu till now, though it was so not that bad like the case of Nero, playing fiddle when the Rome was burning.

I am sure Sir, I am not referring you, because, you are an exception and you have been the first person to receive the blows in all cases of confrontations till now, the big leaders, are likely to survive as they managed till now, to enjoy, in the independent India, the fruits of the efforts and sacrifice of millions of poor innocent patriots who have laid and are going lay their lives for every one of us to get the freedom. Can you assert that those future beneficiaries ever suffered like the majority of the people, when the struggle for independence was intensified after your arrival from South Africa under your leadership? Sir, history is replete with thousands of cases where the Kings and even the Emperors had courageously participated in the wars along with the soldiers right from the days of Arjuna, the hero of the Epic Mahabharatha, many of them were killed and they considered death in the battle fields, as a virtue of a Brave ruler. But the advocates of democracy demanding the abolition of Monarchy and foreign rule, have they ever followed the golden rule in their encounters with the British, till date? Have they not remained at a safer distance in far off places and used their tongue and pen powers instead- to condemn the attacks or condole the massacres or butchery of the innocent- or write articles against the British instigation or atrocities, particularly when the communal clashes take place between the innocent Hindus and Muslims, who have been living peacefully for centuries with out a rift till the advent of the political interference?

Permit me to say Sir political leaders, barring you and a few others, always survived and will survive, with out any personal physical attacks, after sacrificing the soldiers of democracy, to finally enjoy the fruits of the sacrifices. According to me, they are worse than the Monarchs .

I feel that democracy is an ingenious method of enjoying the powers of the Kings and at the same time, with out risking personal life of the kinglike leaders in all the encounters with the enemies. That is the reason why many Indians have joined after 1930s and are joining the Congress, at this stage of struggle, to become leaders to share the spoils.

There may be many exceptions to my statements - but all those exceptions have already sacrificed their lives and perished in the process of getting the ultimate ruling power for the vested interest. But sir, you are the only leader who remains till now, and would remain for ever with out ever nurturing the thought of power, I can boldly proclaim in the open forum, because I know you, now.

Sir, please take the jail life of the leaders, for example. It is not a bed of roses and it is a hell but Sir, have you ever suffered like the imprisoned ordinary party workers that much even in the jail, except in the beginning of your political career? Are you not kept in a palace even now when you are supposed to be undergoing jail sentence? Wont you agree that you, Pandit and important big shots are given a better treatment by the British, even while serving your jail sentences till now? Are they not evidences to prove my assertions –please take for example the case of Jawaharlal Nehru-who holds the records for the longest jail life till now-how could he write volumes during his stay in prisons, to his daughter? Why was he not given work like other prisoners of freedom struggle? Why did he not refuse to accept a differential treatment for him ? Did he think that he was superior to common patriots ? Was he not a common Indian like other crores of people living all over the country? Then why did he not insist that all the prisoners arrested and jailed under the freedom struggle should be given the same privileges like him- to remain comfortably in his well maintained cell writing poems and letters to all their children. Finally, why did you not refuse the same differential treatment given to you now ? Are you not aware of the patriots languishing in Indian jails, eating rotten food, wearing checked and numbered dresses, working like animals and treated worse than animals?"

Again, Chandru stopped, expecting a slap or two from the great saint like man. Instead, he saw , only tears dropping down through the extended moustache on his wrinkled cheeks. Chandru thought that he had wounded his feelings. He immediately fell on his feet. Holding them, in his palms, he cried-seeking his pardon for his impertinence.

But Gandhiji recovered quickly from his sudden emotional disturbance, lifted the face of Chandru, with difficulty as he was not still very weak after the recent illness, and told him,

" Chandru, you should have been the first person I should have met after my return to the nation. But everything has already happened and they are irreversible and has become past now. I have already told you, in the beginning of your stay with me that I would not answer your questions or approve or contradict your views. But today, I am making an exception with your permission. I admit that I have done a terrible mistake in accepting the special treatment for

44

me, while undergoing the jail sentences till now. No one including Ba had ever pointed out the sin I have been committing in remaining comfortable even after being imprisoned in palaces and special cells in the jails. I as the leader, should have undergone the same torture like the common patriots. But it not too late even now- I will demand my transfer to an ordinary jail cell immediately, Chandru, though, you will not be permitted to stay with me. You can come and see me as per the jail rules common to all patriots. At least from now on, I am going to strive hard to come up to your expectation of a true patriot and a leader"- it was Gandhiji who was holding the hands of Chandru then- looking at him with an expectation.

Chandru could not stand the stand taken by his great leader. He stood up and with a look of determination, he addressed the path finder of freedom struggle:

" sir, if you ever try to move away to a simple prison cell now at this stage, I will not be alive to see you there. I will go to my mother and tell her that I have failed in my mission once again. Sir, it is too late for you to decide for you. You are a national property. You are the life of millions. You may be willing to suffer – you will not be allowed to by your supporters- including the great Panditji and Patel. You wanted my candid views with out fear or favour- the famous Indian idiom I suppose, about many things- I have told you as per your instruction. But that does not mean that you would react immediately and take a decision which would sidetrack the main issue of the struggle for freedom. Suppose you insist or go on fast till you are kept with other common patriots, what the British would do? You are now an internationally famous leader. Neither they can put you in C class jail and see you suffer nor can they leave to your end by fasting. In the meantime, your Panditji and others might raise hue and cry in the nation and there would bedlam everywhere, congressmen suspecting ill-treatment of their leader in the palace by the innocent British, demonstrations, lathe charges, shoot to kill orders and a few deaths, and finally you are back to a much more comfortable palace. Do you want all of us to perish Sir? Do you want some more killings ? Hereafter I will not tell my views if they are going to upset your noble mind and create unwanted confusion in the task taken up to drive away the British from out land."

When Chandru finished talking, Gandhiji asked him to take rest for the day as he has lot of things to do from the next day.

****

Tail end piece: Chandru was introduced to all the Congress committee members as an observer on 6th May 1944, by Gandhiji after his unconditional release by the British. But Panditji was visibly not happy to have some one between him and Babuji. Right from the beginning, he was simply ignoring Chandru, though, Chandru was getting along well with Patel. Others were confused over the role of Chandru who was neither a member nor an outsider as he appeared to be too close to Gandhiji. Hence, they neither ignored him nor moved with him closely. Chandru acted an observer to the core, simply be present when ever Gandhiji asked him to be present and observe.

He was the luckiest person to tour Bengal and Assam, with Gandhiji in Dec 1945 and Jan 1946. While he was accompanying him during the tour of South India in Jan and Feb 1946, undertaken particularly, for the purpose of propagating the removal of the untouchability and establishing a national link, Gandhiji openly praised the South Indians for their courage and patriotism. With out telling the background of Chandru, he introduced him, as one such daring lion from the caves of South India. Wherever he went, he told openly that Chandru was his politically adopted son who would continue his(Gandhiji's) work after him. The local congressmen and leaders were surprised to see Chandru for the first time with Gandhiji. But on seeing his closeness with their leader, they started respecting the stranger, but with a question mark in their minds.

On June 18th 1946, Chandru was introduced the proposal for including Chandru as a member in the Congress Working Committee which was held to decide about the acceptance of Interim Government scheme. Others in the committee were all taken aback for the unexpected addition in the agenda of the meeting. Panditji known for his temper, quickly asked Gandhiji,

" Babuji, is it so important now to take up the case of membership to your personal assistant. We are here to decide an important issue of very high national importance. But you have chosen this time to seek membership of this person who is not known to any other members here leave alone the millions of patriotic congress party workers like him. Please allow me to commence the work on the agenda"

Gandhiji simply smiled and asked " Pandit. do you still have faith in me and my love for the country? "

Nehru and others present in the meeting were flabbergasted by the question.

" Babuji, what nonsense are you talking? How can you ever ask me whether I have faith in you? Who am I to question your love for us and the country? Babuji, please give me some other punishment and not the punishment by words" Nehru's words really shook the members including Gandhiji, who was sitting only next to Nehru, simply hugged him with his right hand. He pacified and cooled down his tempers simply by his affectionate hugging with out uttering a single word.

"Pandit, please do not misunderstand my words. I have never doubted the mutual trust and love we have between us. and I would not do in future also. But here I want to explain something else. I cannot postpone this any longer. This political genius,(pointing out to Chandru)unfortunately is unable to come out in the open, for reasons you and I , besides Patel only knew. He should have been taken as our political advisor right from the begging of our struggle. But it is too late to think about that at this stage. But I am not going to keep quiet now when we are here to decide about our acceptance of the interim government. Let me take the privilege of recommending him as a member of the working committee . I want one of you to second it. Then we are having the right to get the benefit of his excellent advice or at least his sharp criticisms on the decisions we take from now, till we establish our own government based on our own constitution.

Pandit, he is not my assistant. He is my political adviser with retrospective effect. He had opened my eyes on several issues and pointed out the mistakes I had made unintentionally. He is one hundred percent a freedom fighter like you, me and others present. He has travelled for five years, by foot and has seen the conditions prevailing in each and every village of the country and knows the views of the people better than any one in this august gathering. So, may I ask for a favour from you all in the national interest? Please admit him as a member straight away as he holds already a full-fledged congress membership from 1930. Finally, you need not respect him as your equal but at least respect him as a fellow Indian. The political intelligence and patriotic feelings are not our exclusive rights. Outside this room, there are millions of patriotic citizens who are more knowledgeable, capable and result-oriented in their approach than us. But for reasons we do not know they are not here. Chandru is one of them, who is here. I leave it to you to decide this issue first before going to the national level decision."

Gandhiji looked around to find out how the senior members of the congress had taken his opinions about the admission of the new member. Patel suddenly said that he seconded the proposal of Gandhiji for admitting Chandru as the member of the working committee. Others in chorus endorsed the admission and Nehru, a gentleman to the core, declared that Chandru had become a full fledged working committee member from then on. Chandru neither smiled nor remained morose. But others congratulated him. He thanked them all. Thereafter the national issue was take up and was decided to accept the interim government scheme.

On April 12, 1947, Gandhiji had informed Lord Mountbatten that his plans to make Jinnah as the First Prime Minister of the undivided India, had not been accepted by the Congress Party and hence, he would not be involved personally in any further negotiations, which would be taken up only by the congress committee thereafter.

PRIVATE DISCUSSIONS WITH GANDHIJI
-3-

On 25/5/1947, Gandhi said " In the India that is shaping today there is no place for me- I have no wish to live".

8 months 5 days, before Gandhiji was shot by Ghotse brothers, Gandhiji was looking very tired. The freedom " was not won- but given-" Gandhiji was lamenting. " If only we have won, there should not have been a Pakistan and Hindustan" he was telling Chandru.

" I wanted you to be in the new government. But you have resigned from the congress committee after I wrote the letter to Mountbatten, about my decision not to participate in any further negotiations.

48

That was done, with out consulting me. At least you should have remained with the Pandit to guide him and advice him as you did for me, instead following me like my shadow, fasting with me, walking with me everywhere, be an observer in the meetings addressed by me, acting like my body guard when I ventured to go and see all those people affected by the communal violence, in the riots torn-North and East of the country.

The result- now you have no place in the new government with your village based approach, like me. You are also stuck with me, with your ideals, declining the offer from Panditji, to take a ministerial post in the new government, unlike Patel, who had opted for the second position. We two have become the spent force. I sincerely wish, that Pandit with his modern socialistic approach would solve the basic problems of the 38 crores Indians in the divided Hindustan"

Looking at Chandru, he said suddenly as if he thought about the subject just then

" it is long time since you and I had time like today. Events that had taken place one after another till now, had never allowed us to think about anything else. You have not spoken to me for a long time. Today, I am in the mood to hear you. Tell me everything you want to say. Do not keep something for a next time- who knows that the next time may not come for ever".

(The very prophecy of a saintly person like Gandhiji, came true with in a month when he was killed foolishly by a fanatic.)

Chandru before narrating what he had in his mind requested Gandhiji not to make such undesirable statements about his future. He said ,

" Master, you would certainly live for many more years with robust health, as the wishes of millions of poor Indians would prevent him from leaving the terra firma as this crucial stage when their future is at stack in the hands of the newly formed government".

Then he began:

" I am asking you, Sir, during the period of 500 years of Muslim domination and rule, in our country, how many times the country had Noakhali type of massacres? How many Hindus were killed just because of Muslim oppression? Here we should not take into account the deaths in the war fields, at the time of invasion by the Muslim Kings when they fought with the fragmented Hindu Kingdoms. If the Hindu Kings were united, the question of Muslim kingdoms was ruled out. But for, the meek and selfish Kings, who were more in numbers , ruling the country at that time, the invading Moguls wouldn't have found it easier to establish their empire. By taking one at a time with their mighty army with cannons, they established their supremacy in the alien land, easily. But during the rule of Great Mogul emperors, there was no widespread hatred for Hindus and there were no recorded human massacres of Hindus; the two religions were existing side by side and people irrespective of their religious followings were living whether happily or prosperously , it is irrelevant , because even now they are peacefully co-existing, with all their day to day problems.

The point is that Muslim domination during Mogul rule had not oppressed, the Hindus as per History, forcing them to raise up against the Moguls like what they have done against a mightier British Empire from the middle of nineteenth century. In either case, the invaders and rulers were foreigners. Since there was no recorded struggle for independence during Muslim rule, it is safe to conclude the anti Muslim feeling in the Hindus and the anti Hindu feelings in the Muslims were all the making of the political leaders who thrived during the freedom struggle with out being seriously affected, unlike the middle level and lower level or gross root level ordinary freedom fighters, who had to shed their lives or rot in the hell-like jail cells. None of the top leaders faced the torture like the ordinary freedom fighters; You, Sir and Pandit Nehru were in jail for long – Panditji had time to write big volumes of letters to his daughter. But did they suffer like other freedom fighters of lower standing, butchered by the British jail officials, police personnel, or the British armed forces?

How many leaders were killed by the police? How many congress leaders died during the famine of the Bengal ? How many members of the Congress party died during the Hindu Muslim massacres? I do not know. Right from the formation of a political party till now , can any one tell how many leaders had sacrificed their life for the cause of the people?

You were totally obsessed with the idea of Unified India ; if only you have seen pragmatically, all the blood sheds could have been avoided. Sir you played into the conspiracy of Churchill and Mountbatten who wanted chaos and disorder between the Hindus and Muslims. There was no nation before the advent of British traders in India It was all the making of the British over the two hundred years. As you have rightly said that the independence was conferred on us and not won by us In fact it was Great Briton who took the brunt of consolidating the small kingdoms by sacrificing their troops and at their cost, of course and by playing safely the divide and rule policies. We are in a way indebted to them, am I correct Sir?

But India as we have today in 1947- is the benign creation of the foreign rule; but for the outsiders with so much strength and money, no Indian could have fought over the disintegrating Mogul empire in the seventeenth century; even if some one tried, the result would have been the emergence of another empire of some dynasty but there is no question of democracy for the Indians or for the people of hundreds of erstwhile states.

Before the advent of the British, there were only sovereign kingdoms and the Mughal empire, controlled by Muslim- kings. Hence permit me o say, Sir, you should have realized the impracticality of containing or keeping the entire Muslim and Hindu population under one banner when the Muslims political middlemen were after power to rule the Muslim dominated areas like the Hindus who were after the whole lot of Muslims and Hindus. You have unfortunately failed to realize for a moment that you are a Hindu and if you wanted the Muslims to be united and be a minority in the unified nation, are you not expecting all the Muslims to be like you, interested only in an Unified Nation.

Sir, allow me to say, you have not thought about the future of the country after uniting the Muslims and Hindus- the nation has to be administered on day to day basis from Peshawar to NEFA and Kashmir to Kanyakumari, now after the freedom. I feel, sir, it is Prudential blessing that the two culturally different heterogeneous groups of leaders have parted way a few months before on 15th August of this year.

You are not correct in adamantly sitting on the issue of unifying the two religious communities, when the innocent Hindus and Muslims are being poisoned by the politicians, from 1905, for achieving their individual goals of getting powers to rule the land. Earlier to the advent of Muslim/Hindu political movement, the ordinary Hindus and Muslims were living peacefully cursing their own fate and living with their day to day problems which were common to both. They had no time or money, to worry about others as the major part of their lives were spent for survival. I declare –" **It was the leaders in the name of fighting for freedom for the country from the foreign rule, who had sown the seeds of religious hatred among the otherwise peace loving people during the earlier Mughal rule"**
.

If Hindus and Muslims were fighting always even before the 1946 tragedies, then the blame would not go to the political leaders. But the entire carnage, drama or the hue and cry for independent Pakistan and the unified Hindustan were the making of the selfish politicians. They first fuelled the hatred between the sober groups of Hindus and Muslims giving the cock and bull story about oppressions and exploitation for the minority group. Later taking advantage of the blood baths - they managed to plant the idea in the minds of the innocent people the urgent need for demanding separate entity for the two religious groups.

I do not deny the fact that back in the mind of a few unselfish politicians or the so called freedom fighters, prior to or at the time of the communal clashes there could have been the avaricious ideas of uplifting the lot of their kin But like you, sir, from Hindustan, there was no such powerful saintly Muslim leader against the partition. Jinnah though he was having serious illness, never gave up his demand for a " moth eaten Pakistan". With the result, the hapless poor Muslims and Hindus paid a very costly price- laying their lives in thousands because of the noble mistake of a saintly person like you- Sir, only you were against the partition when the Hindu and Muslim leaders along with the British Viceroy were all for the two independent states.

Had you realized that it was only your lonely individual wish not to divide the country- into Pakistan and Hindustan, the human massacres everywhere, could have been averted. **You have forgotten that you were not an Emperor to expect your wishes to become law- you were and now also , you are an ordinary citizen, after all, one among the million Indians, under democratic set up. Were you expecting "unification" as a price for the efforts taken by you for getting the freedom ? or were you thinking that all your efforts would become meaningless if the country was divided? You can only reply, sir, if you want.**

But one thing I am very sure that you would not have insisted on your personal wish to be given so much importance. But, sir, what had happened had happened and despite the adamant insistence on Unification of the two religion based lands by you, the partition did take place and thousands were sacrificed meaninglessly by the commitment of an unintentional crime by a noble soul like you - **in Tamil there is a proverb- no one would put even a diamond needle in his eyes. I still do not know whether you were considered as a diamond needle during the period of partition?**

If Jinnah and Panditji think that Pakistanis and Indians, living under the mercy of the kings for thousands of years, are capable of suddenly electing their rulers, after knowing the conditions and the mindsets of the majority village based poor illiterate, all these years, even if you throw me out I would still say " **they are unfit to have fought freedom for the poor illiterate millions**. They are undoubtedly wrong in expecting -

1   the illiterate Pakistanis and Indians, majority of them living in villages, under abject poverty, would be in a position to analyse the situations and start exercising their franchise to elect their rulers, immediately after freedom

2   the future rulers would be as selfless as they are now and
The poor millions struggling to survive on a day to day basis, who are eagerly expecting their food, shelter, clothes and water, for hundreds of years, would come forward to learn first, forgetting their other life saving problems,

To select the right kind of rulers and who would, in turn, develop the independent India and Pakistan to become   self sufficient peaceful nations in the world.

Sir, does it not sound too much to expect from the people, for whom the freedom is only a word, whether it is in English or Hindi or Urdu? Can you tell me Sir, whether their basis problems have been solved after August 15th of
this year?

Then what difference does it make whether they are under X ruler or Y ruler as   long as they have no solutions for   their perennial problems for centuries?

Sir, another thing, I observed-the Muslims were watching Nehru's and Patel's tasting powers as politicians in the interim governments at the centre and in the provinces before freedom was given to us? Hence I am of the opinion, correct me if I am wrong, you appear to have neither judged the mindsets of the political power mongers of India nor the minority Muslim leaders' hunger for power to control their clan separately . You are a saint,   an idealist and personification of a selfish soul. .

Despite the fact that the Indian continent was a jungle of contradictions in the fields of religion, language, culture, caste, and administrative styles of the sovereign states, you wanted homogeneity among the people and the political leaders. Particularly, you have erred or mistook or overestimated the congress leaders' dedication, loyalty, patriotism and suitability for ruling the country after forming the government.

Sir, one more mistake you have done, but unintentionally, based on your only wish to have an unified nation. You had stopped Ambedkher from demanding independent land for Harijans. But what happened? The same congress party and the same Hindu leaders who stood with you till you were struggling for freedom, quietly deserted you and could not be controlled by you or did not listen to you or did not obey your wishes, at the last moment of freedom struggle- why sir, because- they are eagerly waiting for power to rule the country after independence, rather than listening to you who is not required by them any more.

Therefore sir, I can conclude with out hesitation , that your vision of starting the govt from the villages might be flown in the wind along with Ambedhkar's vision of guaranteeing a better deal and land for the Harijans.

Sir, though you only galvanized the people of India, activated them, to win freedom but your idea of creating an Independent India has not been given an honest trail. You were building your dreams of starting the rule from the villages but the leaders whom you have relied on, all these years till 1947, to realize your dreams appear to me, as letting you down or simply ignoring you or belittling your wonderful plans of staring the new government from the villages."

On seeing Gandhiji's ashen face, Chandru stopped talking. Gandhiji was simply not there in that room. He was mentally away, drifting into the past. After a few minutes, he simply lied down and with in a few minutes he was fast asleep- a boon he must have got specially for being a political saint.

PRIVATE DISCUSSIONS
WITH GANDHIJI
-4-

On 15/8/1947 when the independence was declared Gandhi was in riot torn Calcutta . He felt that India had gone temporarily mad. " I do not agree with what my closest friends have done or are doing. ... I cannot challenge the present congress leadership and demolish the people's faith in it unless I am in a position to tell them 'here is an alternative leadership. I must therefore swallow the bitter pill". He appeared to be highly agitated and mentally upset.

Chandru knew that Gandhiji had suddenly arranged a press meeting on that day in the evening in that riot torn city, inviting the national and international press persons- but he thought that the press meet was for arranged in connection with the ongoing riots but he never knew that he would become the purpose of the Press Meet. Around 4.55 pm, Gandhiji known for his punctuality appeared in the hall where the venue was arranged by his other assistants, who also remained with him always.

After welcoming the members of the fourth estate warmly Gandhiji, disclosed the purpose of the meet-

" Ladies and gentlemen from the print media,

You are eagerly expecting a sensational announcement or statement from this old man- about the foolish mutual killing, between the members of the same family. All I want to say about the family fights, here, between the Hindus and Muslims, is – by killing your own brethren , you are doing exactly opposite to what you have in your mind. If only you stop and think calmly- you will realize your foolishness in killing- and how you are flouting your own objectives or aims?

Suppose you kill a few Hindus, what happens – they become dead bodies.- a few Hindus less on the earth and is the case with Muslims. Suppose they kill a few Muslims- what happens- they also become dead bodies. But whether both the group of dead bodies know whether they are Muslims or Hindus? Hindus also call them as 'dead bodies' and Muslims also call them 'dead bodies'. So the two groups of dead bodies come under one group-'dead bodies' beyond the care of Muslim and Hindu. When a Muslim kills a Hindu, he does not kill anything called Hindu- he kills a human and when a human is killed, the identity is lost. But the Hinduism lives. The word Hindu and Muslim are names –take for example- Krishna dies- it means a human with the name of Krishna dies- the name does not die. Understand. If the rioting thoughtless mobs realise this truth, there would be no killing. The people in the opposing religious groups,   must allow humans to live- if they want – they are free to kill the religion if they can. A Muslim can become a Hindu and a Hindu can become a Muslim. Hence killing a Hindu or Muslim indicates the loss of the chance to convert a Hindu in to a Muslim or vice versa. All of you know, evolution of human specie. Our ancestors were monkeys and there was and even today there is no Muslim or Hindu monkey. All these religions were introduced between now and the beginning of Human history. So, no one can claim to be a Muslim from the evolution. That common ancestral background should be remembered while pouncing on to kill. Religion was founded to show the path to divinity only and not the path way to death. That must be remembered. If two sets of brain-washed people kill themselves, instigated by their mad leaders, knowing fully well that religion is a platform only for realising the

Allah or Easwar- and not a platform for expressing their hatred between them- that is entirely different- because that is mass suicide. But these mad people kill innocent Muslims and Hindus also– that is what is disturbing me so much. That is all I want to tell about the riots.

But I am pained today to see all my efforts to have an unified nation was frustrated by the cunningness of the British government and the avariciousness of the political leaders from Hindustan and Pakistan. Now what I am going to tell you – is a highly sensational news for you all. All these years, I have safeguarded the secrets waiting for the freedom to come. The time has come All is well in war and love. The British had indulged in violence on a massive scale till they felt satisfied that they had seen enough blood shed of people who had committed no sin except demanding their land for themselves. That has come past history now, in the New India.

Today, I am going to introduce a precious jewel of the freedom struggle- he is an individual like you and me- but with a difference- he was recklessly patriotic- not after I landed in the country- not after the Congress part y was formed- he was a freedom fighter by birth-as a boy of ten he went to the residence of the British offices and abused them in his native tongue- which was not fortunately understood by the officers. He survived but took an oath to learn English to abuse them in their own language so that his abuses would hurt them as their presence had been hurting all the million Indians. That was the patriotic spirit of the boy. He had decided to drive away the foreigners single handed as an 'one man army' from his native place. When he could not get any encouragement for his mission, he heard about me and came to meet me at Sabarmati. Ashram, when he was just nineteen.

I advised him to continue his struggle from his native place and gave a letter to the Provincial Congress party to take the young boy as a member. But I never knew that the boy would retaliate the foreigners in their own style. After he met me in 1930, he contacted me in 1939, when I was in Bombay. When he told me and Ba what he had done during the intervening period was shocking to us. Ba had developed a motherly affection for him right from our first meeting in 1930. I cannot tell you in detail But at least I can give a gist of what he had done daringly with out worrying about his life, but only with a determination to chase the foreigners from his native place"

When Gandhiji stopped for a while, Chandru was looking embarrassed. Only he and Gandhiji knew whom the latter was referring to, since, Gandhiji still not introduced Chandru to the press persons.

Then for about thirty minutes Gandhiji described the events that took place in Pudukottai when Chandru was arrested for attacking an English officer and then about his master plan which he had perfectly executed to destroy all the resident Englishmen in the Palace, and how he had escaped to Bombay slum. Finally he told how he had made the lion-hearted young man to promise him that he would follow non-violence till his end and how Ba had entrusted special tasks of –one- preparing the constitution of the new India, in 1939 itself, and – two- learning to read, write and speak fluently Hindi.

" my dear sirs, for five years, the young patriot, taking our advice and shouldering our tasks, had travelled all over the country, visiting most of the villages, on foot, on bus, on cycle, on train , starving most of the days. eating in those places where free food was given to beggars like him. When his clothes worn out due to constant use, you know, who came to his rescue, beggars like him, who on seeing the wretched conditions of the political beggar, magnanimously parted with their life possessions- old rags in better conditions than the one which was worn by the freedom fighter.

But he loved his foster mother – my wife, Ba so much. When heard that she was dead, he came all the way to Pune, from some remote village Ernakulam, crying throughout the three days of travel, and created such a miserable scene in front of the palace when he was told that Ba's body had already been cremated.- on seeing the plight of the beggar, like me wearing only loin's clothes, the grief stricken beggar was allowed to remain with me.

He has remained with me always-ever since- at a distance –not far away- only observing and not interfering with others who also love me so much like him. I have made him a congress member in 1930 and have recommended him as a working committee member in 1946. But when I relinquished my position in the Congress party when my advice was not accepted, he also resigned from the working committee. He has declined the offer of a ministerial berth in the new government offered by Panditji. He stays with me, like my shadow – at a distance. He has told me clearly that he would not leave me even he were to be offered the Emperorship of the whole world, because he was not willing to take the risk which he had foolishly taken for his mother. The idiot wants to be with me till I live or if he dies he wants me to be with him.

Are you getting impatient – yes- I can see- Let me have the privilege of introducing my politically adopted son, Ramachandran alias Chandru from Pudukottai- Madras Province. We have identical thinking as for as establishing the new government particularly for the poor millions suffering in the villages of this sub-continent. He is ready with the new constitution for the new India. I am sure that if he gets the right support, he would install a Ram Rajya- my dream for the last thirty years.

So far, he has succeeded in accomplishing all the tasks given to him or taken by him- now I am giving him one more or may be the last task – to form a strong administrative base at this nascent stage, for the country, divided by languages, cultures, north –south feelings, rich and poor, besides, the differences between the high and low classes, educated and uneducated, village and urban, higher and lower castes, Hindu and Muslims etc I am sure that my son would carry out the task successfully and make every Indian-right from the poor villager to the highly sophisticated upper class metropolitan resident.-happy and share the fruits of the freedom equally. Jai Hind"

When presspersons posed some questions regarding the government formed by Jawaharlal Nehru, Gandhiji said that he was not a member of a Congress Political party.

"Already I have advised the leaders to either to disband the Congress or change it as a social organisation. They have not listened to me and the erstwhile congress formed for the purpose of freedom struggle has been continued as the political front. Hence, do not ask any questions regarding my views about something on which I have no controls or interest."

When Gandhiji was asked point blank whether he was planning to form his own style of government through his politically adopted son, Gandhiji replied with out hesitation

"My adopted son has no other interest in anything except remaining with me till my end".

When a reporter from a foreign news paper, wanted to know whether he wanted his adopted son to carry out the task he had given, by forming a new political party and after becoming the Prime minister by contesting and winning the elections or change the present direction of the present Congress political party to achieve his dream of Ram Rajya.

Gandhiji, being a veteran in handling the tricky questions of all sorts of pressmen, simply said ,

" I know my adopted son. He is a better judge to adopt a strategy best suited for him to achieve the results, under the prevailing circumstances."

The press meet ended with a lot of hand shakings and hundreds of flash bulbs blurring the vision of Chandru, who was not able to control his surging emotions. Gandhiji smiled and used him for the first time as his walking stick, for leaving the room. Others who were remaining always with him, congratulated Chandru, as they also, like the press persons, came to know for the first time about the background history of the mystery man who always remained with their leader but kept a safe distance from him. They used to wonder who he was as he neither talked with Gandhiji nor talked to by Gandhiji, in public or in their presence. He was an enigma and an unsolved puzzle for them for years. The whole world came to know about Chandru only when Gandhiji told that he used to discuss with the tall man when they were alone.

That night on 19th Jan 1948, when they about to retire, Chandru asked Gandhiji,

"Sir, may I express my views about what you have done today?"

Gandhiji who normally allowed Chandru to air his opinions freely, for reasons not known to the latter, simply said, "not today , betae. I am really happy after accomplishing a task given to me by Ba. One day, before her death, when we were seriously discussing about the future course of action of the freedom movement, she asked me to hand over the task of forming the new government only to you, as she felt that only you could remove the sufferings of the poor villagers. Though she saw many capable persons, who could complete the task-yet she said that they were after the position and the power which went along with the position. Hence, I feel exhausted mentally today and may I request you to postpone the discussions to some other day?"

So saying Gandhiji started his instant sleep.

PRIVATE DISCUSSIONS
WITH GANDHIJI -5-

27th January 1948- That day Gandhiji visited the Muslim fair in Mehrauli .

When he was about to call it a day, suddenly Gandhiji looked at Chandru who was also preparing to retire, and asked him,

"Ramchand (first and the last time he had deliberately addressed Chandru like that) I owe you something. But I do not want to post pone the debt. Hence, please tell me whatever you have in your mind with out reservation, here and now-please"

Chandru who was not expecting that sudden change of mind from Gandhiji, took a few seconds to recover to request his master-

"Babuji(he also addressed him as Babuji for the first time, unconsciously) is it not time for you to sleep? You had been to the fair and you must be tired. Can't we take up this repayment of the debt on some other day?"

"Na betae- na, do not ask me why ? I want to hear you today- please go on"

Chandru was obliged to begin tell what he had in his mind with out knowing that it was the last personal discussions he had with the great saintly leader.

" Sir, I am not going to give any introduction for the remaining few observations I have made during my extensive on the spot study of the nook and corner of the country. May be I am repeating the same observations or remarks again and again. Please excuse for me such repetitions

According to the opinions of many, the Congress party should have recognized the Muslim League as a political party founded for the welfare and development of the Muslims. It was because, the Moguls ruled the country for 500 years and the British acquired the power only from them. Hence the demand for Muslim representation in the Govt was not unreasonable and the Hindu leaders particularly Nehruji and Patel Sahib's intolerance of Muslim league's prominence was unjustifiable. Further, from the beginning of the nineteenth century, the British regime openly favoured Muslims and encouraged them, while hating the Indians and the freedom struggle. They would have even granted freedom to Muslims earlier, like they had done to Burma in 1935, if only there was a leader like you, sir, in the Muslim league.

Similarly the move of Ambedkher to provide a separate land for the Harijans was put down by your Ahimsa tactics. You should have stood by Ambedkher, now, to see that the Harijans are given true independence not from the foreigners, but from the higher castes of Hindus. But the general feelings are that you have done a mistake in abdicating your position and also leaving the congress party in the hands of the higher castes Hindus to form the government and also to frame the constitution. Many true patriots have reportedly felt in your absence that you should not have left the CWC leaders to decide the fate of the country at this crucial moment, when you know, except a few, most of them, are eagerly waiting for enjoying the position and the power.

You appear to have disappointed and let down the people to whom you have promised that the development of the free India would start from the villages after the independence and that the Harijans would be guaranteed equal status in the society.

Sir on this one count of criticism, you and my mother, have acted as per the expectation of the Political critics, some of them called on you today, concealing their views. There has been a wide de spread criticism - 'why drafting of a prototype of a new constitution based on your promises to the people has not been taken earlier to the Independence, for threadbare study and discussions.? Can I continue what people feel about you sir, verbatim?"

Chandru stopped for a few seconds. On seeing no reaction from Gandhiji, he continued taking silence as a sing of acceptance.

"Sir, I am giving the remarks I heard from your well-wishers who dare not come out with their views in your presence. I am quoting them-

"Gandhi, after realizing that the partition became an inevitable end for the Freedom struggle, should have intervened and given a broad outline for drafting the new constitution of the Free India. What he started he should have completed, because every Indian respected and relied only on him and his involvement. He should not washed off his hands and have allowed Pandit Nehru, Patel, Dr Prasad and Ambedkher to draft the permanent guidelines for the country. Nehruji was communist minded, quick tempered, foreign educated, and an aristocratic man, whose pet theory of socialism was nothing but the reflections of soviet government's anti-imperialistic policies. He had already promised to divide the country on the lines of linguistic majority as a reward for the political support, he was given by the regional leaders, during the struggle. Patel was a strong Hindu action king. He never accepted separate treatment for the minority Muslims. He was the best suited person as a Home Minister to work under some one, stronger than him like Gandhi, who was more balanced in his approaches, with long range view. Others were having their own complexes and weaknesses and hence the only alternative available after 15/8/1947 was to frame a strong unassailable and error free constitution with which neither the weakest Prime Minster should find it difficult to run the government nor the corrupt selfish Prime minister should find it easier to run the Govt as he or she liked" Quote ends Sir.

But sir, we should thank the great visionary – my mother- who had already entrusted the task of preparing the constitution in 1939 itself and now you have the so called prototype based on your dream of Ram Rajya. But the only problem is- the present government is not willing to take it even as a suggestion from the citizen of the free India. Sir, it is painful to learn that the new government is reported to be considering the Irish and Westminster models as the basis for drafting the new constitution, for the country where majority of the people are illiterates poor villagers.

Personally, I fee; that you should have been at the helm of affairs now at this stage of forming a new government and drafting the new constitution. Do you realize that you are leaving the biggest chance, now, to protect the people from the misuse of power by the leaders of the political parties. Sir, now just after independence, **leaders or politicians are amenable to any change, ready to obey or follow any rules, restrictions, duties and responsibilities, because there is no precedence.** India is in the process of becoming a nation, for the first time in the history of the country as we were all along the subjects of Kingdoms under the erratic control of the Monarchs. Hence the time is so ripe, no one but you, can find a very practical people-oriented simple constitution, with the Government functioning from the villages.

I think that the Congress is dominated and controlled by Nehruji – a foreign educated scholar from an aristocratic family moulded by you as a leader- I am sorry to say, no more under your not control. People feel that right from 1930, he(Panditji) was behaving as if he was the Prime minister and wanted his socialist approach to be the national policy of the free India, ignoring the objections by the conservatives. But then sir, you have stood by him- that was observed to be the biggest mistake, done by you. When in 1946, 12 out of 15 provincial congress committees had voted in favour of Patel being elected as Party President, Sir, you had opted for Nehruji to be the Congress President. Hence no one could do anything against the dogmatic and super imposing personality of Nehru who has taken over the task of forming the new government and drafting of the constitution, blatantly deviating from the promises made by you to the millions of people.

Many political observers openly say – " If these leaders earnestly start going to house to house or from village to village to ascertain the public opinion about their new government and the new constitution, they would not have time to pose as leaders. But more than that, they are mortally afraid of one imminent possibility-when they are on their errands, some clever persons would seize the opportunity and try to usurp their position , to participate in negotiations and travel here and there and address gathering of people. Hence till now, all the political leaders right from the beginning of the struggle, except perhaps you sir, addressed people in thousands only and not individually, and tried to mesmerize them or brain wash them, instigate them and use them as pans for fulfilling their personal dreams- in the name of the development of the country for the self development and dynasty rule. Sir, here I am not making any sweeping remarks against many true patriots – who are not clamouring for any political positions of power today. Like the dew drops disappear on seeing the glory of Sun, those true patriots disappeared from the national scene once the freedom was won and the country got its independence !!

One more adverse remark which no one had the courage to make it in your presence, which I forgot to tell your earlier.

In Lahore session , Motilal had passed on the Presidentship of the Congress to his son Jawaharlal with your blessing, making it to appear as a family affair . You have been accused of establishing a dynasty rule in a public movement while demanding the abolishment of monarchy and democracy for people. Did not appear that you were making mockery of democracy which meant every one was equal in the eyes of law?

Similarly, observers feel that the upper class local politicians have already become congressmen. It was but natural. Who can think of spending time and money for political activities not related to day today problems of living? Only the rich, the middle and upper middle classes. Therefore not only now and certainly in future, Congress party is going to depend for its existence and sustenance mainly on Hindu landed peasants at the base, and Parsis crore-pathis at its summit. Which means the priority for the village poor would be seriously affected and pushed to the back seat-and only the needs of the middle and upper classes would be given top priority by the new government.

THE ABRUPT END OF THE PRIVATE DISCUSSIONS

In the early evening hours of 30 January 1948, Gandhi met India's Deputy Prime Minister and his close associate in the freedom struggle, Vallabhai Patel, and then proceeded to his prayers.

That evening, as Gandhi's time-piece, which hung from one of the folds of his *dhoti* [loin-cloth], was to reveal to him, he was uncharacteristically late to his prayers, and he fretted about his inability to be punctual. At 10 minutes past 5 o'clock, with one hand each on the shoulders of Abha and Manu, who were known as his 'walking sticks', Gandhi commenced his walk towards the garden where the prayer meeting was held. As he was about to mount the steps of the podium, Gandhi folded his hands and greeted his audience with a namaskar; at that moment, a young man came up to him and roughly pushed aside Manu. Nathuram Godse bent down in the gesture of an obeisance, took a revolver out of his pocket, and shot Gandhi three times in his chest. Bloodstains appeared over Gandhi's white woollen shawl; his hands still folded in a greeting, Gandhi blessed his assassin: *He Ram! He Ram!*
As Gandhi fell, his faithful time-piece struck the ground, and the hands of the watch came to a standstill. They showed, as they had done before, the precise time: 5:12 P.M.

Chandru who as usual was accompanying his mentor at a distance, heard the gun shots from the crowd, following the Mahatma. who was walking with the support of his usual human walking sticks- the two who were grand daughters of the Gandhiji. When he rushed to check what was the reason for the sudden commotion and the simultaneous melancholic cries of the hundreds of those who had come to pray with their Babuji, he saw the great leader- the political saint, the apostle of peace- the man who preached and followed non-violence and the saviour of the downtrodden and the master of freedom struggle- lying on his back-with bleeding injuries caused by the bullets- fired at close range. **It was a fitting reward for a human soul who won the freedom for a big nation with out shedding a drop of blood – but ironically, the same Mahatma was forced to shed blood – But if some one thought that the freedom could not be won with out blood shed- he proved them wrong- because- he shed his own blood only after he got the freedom for the millions !**

Chandru did not cry, since every one was doing it, uncontrollably. He remembered what Gandhiji told him " I would live in you and help you to establish the Ram Rajya- your body and my soul". He felt that Gandhiji, as a national leader, could not die- because Gandhiji was only a name. But his philosophy, dreams, speeches, the love and affection people have in him, the unforgettable association many had with him, his quick walking, with a stick, wearing a loin's clothing , and a watch hanging from the cavity between the clothing and his hip etc- no one who moved with him could forget. The Harijans and the millions of poor Indians keeping him in their heart were worshipping him . Then Chandru thought – how could he die?

He remained near the spot where Gandhiji was shot, simply looking at it. Panditji was informed and Dy Prime Minster Vallabhai Patel was all ready present. All the leaders and others rushed with the body to the hospital .Gandhiji had become a state property and the government had taken charge of further proceedings as per the protocol. Chandru knew that he had no place near the slain hero of the freedom struggle, when Panditji was in charge of the government. Hence, he had decided to stay back at the place where his master breather his last.

Police came and requested Chandru to leave the place as they had taken charge of the place. Prostrating before the spot where he was shot, Chandru quietly walked away from the garden, but not knowing where should he go. He had no place in the big city which he could call his own. Ever since he came running to see the dead body of his mother, in Pune in 1944, he was with the Mahatma. Since he had gone, leaving him alone, though the world looked so empty- yet, he had no place- what an irony - Chandru walked as his legs could carry him. The rudder of his life-boat- had gone- though the engine was just alive- . He was neither a boat nor an oar. Throughout the night, he was walking and in the early morning when he felt that he could no longer walk, he lied down and slept on the pavement outside the bungalow of an ICS officer, in charge of defence.

When he heard faintly that someone was shouting at him, Chandru opened his eyes and saw the Police men standing over him and demanding explanation from him for sleeping on the platform outside the residence of the government officer. Chandru was mentally bankrupt- the death of his master had squeezed all his strength and left him as a human shell. Hence when the policemen wanted explanations he could not immediately give it. But that delay irritated them who deployed brutal force to shake Chandru with a few blows on his cheeks. Only on the previous evening the Mahatma was shot dead by some assailment. They were terribly afraid of everything- started looking at every one with suspicion. So when they saw a crumpled figure of a middle aged person sleeping on the pavement outside an important government official, they had to naturally become cautious and that was what they had done. They took Chandru who had not recovered from his hazy semi-conscious state, to the Parliament Police station. But when the station in charge saw the suspect, he shouted at the two police patrol men for having brought a person who was openly introduced as his adopted son by Mahatma himself. He immediately brought some water and called the doctors nearby while informing the Home department about the conditions of Chandru.

Everything happened in a lightning speed. Chandru was taken to General Hospital , where he was given immediate drips and medicines. With in a short while, Vallabhai Patel came and saw Chandru who had regained his consciousness but remained spiritless. He was asking Chandru to take the loss in his stride and promised to come back after ,making arrangements for every one to pay their   last minutes respects to the departed soul.

From where they got the information, Chandru did not know- a few press persons were arguing with the hospital staff insisting on meeting him. On hearing the commotion very near the room where he was lying, with the bottle of saline water attached to his wrist , he asked the nurse to let them in.

With a big 'namathe' three reporters walked in smiling. Once the formal introduction etc were over, they wanted to know how he had taken the loss of the Mahatma.

" My dear sirs, please correct your statement - my master has only deserted the body in which he was residing as per the genetic science. But he can never die or disappear. As long as me and millions of poor Harijans and villagers are alive , guarding him carefully in her thoughts and deeds – no divine power can take him away from us, leave alone the gun shots of a mad man. Particularly after he was forced to shed his mortal remains he has attained immortality in the minds of you, me and very Indian alive and going to be born in this land for ever. With out knowing the truth of his ubiquitous nature of existence, the idiots had killed one Gandhiji- are they going to or can they ever kill the millions of people who are Gandhiji's by their thoughts and deeds found every nook and corner of the country? Sirs, can you refute my statements?"

The press team was amazed by the reply and the unshakable faith Chandru had in the slain leader. One of them asked :

" Sir, we heard that you have been left when Gandhiji was taken to hospital and you walked away aimlessly –sleeping on a platform, arrested by policemen on patrol and later brought here by the intervention of the Dy. Prime Minister- is it a fact?"

Chandru smiled " first of all your question itself was not correct. It was not for a function Gandhiji was rushed to the hospital. There was no question of some one left or some one included. It was a crisis. I chose to remain on the spot where my soul-mate breathed his lost. I was warming up with his breath- I felt that his soul must be there waiting for me to be alone. I did that. But the police guard requested me to leave. I left – I have no home of my own. Hence I just wandered till I felt exhausted. I never knew that I slept on a platform. The patrolling police had done their duty and at the police station, the officer thought that it was his duty to inform the higher ups and here I am – recovering from the physical exhaustion. But no authority or medicine can activate my dead spirits- I am not mourning - because – the saint made it clear to me- "Chandru- now we are two separate bodies and two different souls –mentally merged with   after my death also there would be no change-we will be two souls and one body- you will have to carry my soul also".

The presspersons did not know what to ask a person speaking more like a philosopher than like a politician. Finally they asked:

" Sir, we respect your sentiments. But please tell us clearly, are you going to join the government to bring the Ram Rajya in the country?"

Chandru suddenly became tensed, when he replied emphatically,

"Yes-the only task before me is to make the dreams of my master come true- that too- very shortly. I would not hesitate to take any steps to accomplish the tasks given to me by my mother through my master. If necessary , I would not hesitate to involve the people in attaining my goal."

The reporters got what they wanted. They were happy that they had enough ammunition for crating sensational news on the next day morning. They thanked and left happily. Chandru who was a novice in handling the press persons did not know what he had done by his emotional outburst.

It was Birla house. There was a very big queue of mourners, signing the favourite songs of the Mahatma- *Raghupathi Raghava Rajaram.. Vaishnava jananatho…* moving along slowly towards the place where the remains of the great leaders was laid in state. Flower and hand spun cotton yarn garlands and wreaths galore Gandhiji was facing the heaven with his eyes closed, but his unselfish service to the nation remained ever in the minds of the millions When Chandru was brought to the Brittle house as per the instruction of Patel, he got down well before the destination and joined the queue of the mourners, turning down the request of the personal secretary of the Dy. Prime Minister, to come with him directly to the VIP enclosure, where Patel was waiting for him.

Singing the song of the Mahatma along with others, Chandru was thinking about his long association with the leader and his wife. With out his physical efforts, the queue brought him to the place where Gandhiji was kept for public to pay their homage. He stood before the slain leader who believed that he would live for 125 years for a few minutes and then collapsed like a pack of cards. On seeing Chandru coming along with the general public, Panditji signalled Patel asking why he was not brought directly to the special enclosure. When Patel was conveying to Nehru what he heard from his Personal secretary told him, Chandru had collapsed at the feet of the Mahatma. His hands were at the feet of the Mahatma. The sons, close relatives of Gandhiji, senior leaders of congress party, and foreign diplomats were all taken aback when a person fainted at the feet of the deceased leader.

Chandru was immediately rushed to the hospital from where he was brought by Patel who wanted Chandru should also see the mortal remains of the leader he was cremated on that day at Jamuna banks. He did it with good intentions, but he never thought that Chandru was upset to such an extent to faint in public, on seeing the remains of the great leaders.

Thus when Gandhiji was cremated, the one person who was missing was his so called political advisor Chandru. But when he regained his conscience and became normal around 3 am in the early morning, he asked why he was in the hospital when he should be with his master. The nurse who knew Chandru, politely told him that he should wait till the morning when he could get the information he wanted from the doctor. But on being pestered by the patient, nurse contacted her matron, who contacted the doctor on duty. But whether to convey the news of cremation to Chandru who was already affected by the death of the Mahatma , no one could decide. It was because, they knew, why, the whole nation knew, through the new papers and the officers of Dy. Prime Minister that the patient was introduced by Gandhiji himself at Calcutta, as his politically adopted son and his successor. Hence the hospital authorities were worried –whether to tell or not to tell the truths. Then they contacted the government officials and who when they did not know what to tell the hospital, finally woke up and told Patel himself.

Finally it he who came personally and carefully unfolded the truths.

"Patel Saheb, when my mother, Ba, died, I could not see her joining the heaven through the medium of flames. Sir, told me to remain with him from then, so that I should not miss the chance, again , in his case. But what happened. I had all the chances and your help. But I could not see the body merging with the heavenly flames." Chandru's voice became diffused and remote.

Patel patted him and asked him to get up- " you have a duty to your master. Babuji has already told me about the task he had given to you. To achieve the task, you should be strong and keep his Ram Rajya as your goal and work for it, from now. Come on. We have a condolence meeting at the Parliament . Come with me" so saying he made Chandru to get up. But Chandru wanted to go Gandhiji's last camp site first, where he had kept his few belongings. After collecting them, he said that he was ready to be shifted to any place in the nation.

Patel took him to his official quarters at   1, Aurangzeb Road in Delhi — this would be his residence till his death in 1950,   along with a medium sized rusty tin sheet box belonging to Chandru. Refusing the help from others, Chandru carried the box and accompanied Patel. There he was introduced to the family members of the Dy Prime Minister. Then he was taken to a very bog room, where there was a big ornamental cot with mattress, along a complete range of furniture to augment the comforts of the occupant. Chandru was hesitating to remain there when Patel asked him to get ready for the prayer.

It was the first time, Chandru entered the mammoth round shaped red marble building- a feast to the eyes of a commoner like him. On the way, many persons not known to him had greeted him, shook hands with him and wished him. But Chandru tagged along the Dy PM, and entered the astonishingly spacious hall- where many senior leaders of the congress, were found, silently waiting for the Panditji and the President to come to come.

There was total silence when Jawaharlal Nehru entered in white famous white Kurtha and Pyjamas. With a few seconds the President also arrived.

The official condolence message was then read by the President and five minutes silence was observe by those who had assembled in that great hall.

Thereafter, a very big oil painted portrait of the Mahatma was unveiled in the central hall of the Parliament. One by one, the leaders went to the spot where the Mahatma had taken a reincarnation in the form of an oil painting and from a big brass bowl readily kept with lot of flowers, took a handful and just dropped them at them, at the feet of the great unselfish-soul, smiling from the canvas.

The protocol was maintained –first the president- then family members of Gandhiji, the Prime Minster, Dy Prime minister, and other ministers, others in the order. But Patel had asked Chandru to come with him and took his turn after the Dy. PM. None except Patel noticed a small furrow on the face of the Prime Minister, but he ignored it.

Once the condolence meeting was over, Patel told Chandru that there was a meeting of the ministers at the Prime Minister Chamber. He asked Chandru to wait in the lounge outside the Prime Ministers office in the Parliament. After an hour's time, the ministers one after another emerged from the PM's chamber and on seeing Chandru seated in the lounge, just ignored him and left. Finally, Patel came straight to Chandru and asked hi whether he would like to see the PM.

When Chandru expressed his willingness, Patel took him inside the very big hall like chamber where there was very long table with a row of chairs on either side. On the extreme end of the table, sat the PM. When Chandru was brought in, he stood up to welcome him and asked him to come and occupy the chair next to him on his left side and Patel taking the chair on the right side.

"Yes, Ramchand, I hope you have recovered from the shock though you can never recover from the loss. That is human life" he was half smiling when he tried to pacify the person whom he personally neither liked nor disliked at that moment. Nehruji was pained to read the news about the announcement of Gandhiji from Calcutta about Chandru- a rank outsider to the political scene of the nation. But, he did not give too much of importance to it as his relationship with

Gandhiji himself was not that smooth after the partition and the after effects of the Hindu Muslim conflicts created by the partition.

"Sir, I have a letter for you from the master which he told me to give it to you, in case he dies before me"- so saying he gave the closed envelope to Nehru.

.Patel was surprised as he was not aware of any such letter as the fact of it was disclosed to him by Chandru. But he kept quiet, but decided to find out the reason for not informing him about the letter later, when was alone with Chandru.

Quickly Nehru tore open the cover and went through the contents. There was no change in his facial expression. But he simply unfolded it and gave to Patel , who after reading it, smiled at Chandru and gave it back to his PM.

"Ramchand- I am glad to learn that you are a political genius in the opinion of Babuji. But we have many leaders like you with us- who are highly matured, experienced and knowledgeable in the political fields- besides they have sacrificed their life for the nation till now. I understand that you have also undergone many difficulties, sacrificing your life for the struggle. But managing the affairs of a nation, streamlining the working of a government, developing the economy, establishing peace and harmony among the people who had been hitherto living under the control of foreigners' rules, are very difficult tasks which if you claim you have mastered and are holding a model constitution suitable for our Hindustan , I have my sympathies for you. You are not familiar with any one in the country or abroad. You are unknown to the Muslim Leaders- You have no political credential except the one conferred on you- which is not tenable in a democratic country. There are thousands of young patriots like you are eager to take over the government having dreams like you to develop the nation into a highly flourishing economy. I welcome them all to try and accomplish the task- not like you- trying to shoot up to the top floor with the recommendation of a great leader. Tomorrow I can introduce a person like you – why- our Sardar can do the same thing. Like that, we may get hundreds of proposals for doing the best for the nation. They only reflect the interest and involvement people have in building up the nation and nothing else beyond that.

So, Ramchand my best wishes for you to start a political career. Go back to your native place . Since you are already a congress member, you can establish and develop the party at your place. IF you have a good public support, the party high command at the state level may recommend your name for the first Parliament election of the nation which will be held once the formalities of finalizing the draft constitution are over. Then you can make your suggestions about the constitutional changes which would be taken up for discussions on merits. I hope – you have understood the right path to reach the summit. Is there anything else you wish to speak to me?"

Nehruji was about to stand up. Chandru again took out another envelope from his pyjamas pocket and handed over the same to the PM.

Nehruji was visibly upset to see a second cover. Muttering some thing inaudible to Patel and Chandru- he tore open it and read the contents. "Nonsense" he shouted and collapsed in his seat holding the letter in his hand. Patel not knowing what to do, gently asked Nehru whether he could also read the letter. Without a word, Nehruji just extended the hand holding the letter to Patel who took it and read the contents.

He was also shocked. Chandru was puzzled and he wanted to read the letter .On seeing the question mark of confusion on the face of Chandru, Patel himself gave the letter to him.

"Dear Pandit,

I know by now you would have taken your decision and conveyed the same to Chandru. It is difficult for you to accept the truth that the young man knows more than us. I have gone through the text of his constitutional model. They are quite pragmatic –easy to implement- takes the future generation of the leaders also into consideration. He is better than us in many ways. He is twenty years ahead of us in political thinking. He has seen most of the villages in the nation. He had discussed with the people, local leaders, patriots and others. He had given the true picture of the state of affairs prevailing in the nook and corner of the country. He had opened my eyes on many issues on which I was having different opinions- I thought I was taking the right course of action in the freedom struggle. But he proved me wrong on many counts.

Panditji he should have joined us after I landed in the country. But then he was just ten year old boy at that time- but still he started fighting against the British.

Now, that, you have taken your decision, better know the decision we have taken when I found that I would not be able to fulfil the promises, I made to the people, during the freedom struggle, through the Congress party . You have not only declined my request to disband the congress as it had already served its purpose, but converted it as the political party for the sake of forming the new government. Hence, I have entrusted the task of fulfilling my promises to the poor villagers and the illiterates forming majority of the population, to Chandru.

Accordingly, we have formed a political party in the name of JANATA CONGRESS –in which I made Chandru as the first servant of the people. A person who is equally experienced like me in the freedom movement would head the political party. Chandru would approach that person at the appropriate time . Hence, if you cannot give a try for his constitutional model or if you cannot accept him as your political adviser, he will have no other go except to register the party with a letter I have given to him separately, addressing the people to help him for fulfilling my promises and also for establishing my dreams of Ram Rajya. Jai Hind"

There was utter silence in the big hall. Nehru sat crumpled like pack of soiled clothes. Patel was resting on the back of the thick cushion chair, closing his eyes and Chandru was sitting silently looking at the two great leaders. Suddenly Nehruji stood up.

" Ramchand if that is the way Babuji wanted, I have no objection. You carry out his instructions and let me go in my own way to achieve his dreams and fulfil his promises to the poor villagers. But I cannot be cowed down to accept your constitutional model by coercion or threats. Whether you win or we win, ultimately it is Babuji who would become the winner. Good luck" so saying with out even turning to the side of Patel he simply left the chamber in a hurry.

Patel after a few minutes got up and came around to the side where Chandru was sitting frozen by the words of the Prime Minister. He just patted him and said, "do not worry. I will talk to him. Now, you get up . Let us go home and discuss about the matter".

When Chandru was following the Dy. PM , to the waiting car, a few reporters started questioning him regarding the changes if any in the offing after the death of the leader. Patel simply asked them to tell him whether they were expecting changes at that time of national mourning.

At home, after a light break fast, Chandru was met by Patel. His very first question was about the letters.

"Patel Saheb. Gandhiji had told me specifically, **in case he dies before me**, to handover the two covers one by one to Panditji only and I am having one more closed cover which should be given to you after the second letter to Panditji- and that too- only when I am alone with you" so saying he opened the rusty box and took the cover and handed over to Patel.

When Patel read it, he sat down quietly and started looking at the ceiling, ignoring Chandru who was looking at him eagerly.

After some time, he shook his head as if he was replying to some questions, and then looked at Chandru.

"Hare(in Hindu) betae, why are you standing like that? Sit down. Yeh thou kya giya inhonae? (What is this- he has done like this?- in Hindi). Chandru, do you know the contents of this letter?" asked Patel.

Chandru replied ," Patel Saheb- I carry out the instructions of Babuji and only when he asked me to do some thing, I would do. On my own I did nothing after I stayed with him"

"Then read this. Panditji is already upset on seeing the second letter and this letter would make him jump to heavens, I am sure"- he handed over the letter to Chandru.

" Dear Sardar,

This closed letter was meant to be delivered to you only after my death. I know-Chandru would do exactly what I asked him to do.

You know I am not happy with the changes that took place after the decision to hand over freedom to us. Partition did take place whether I liked or not. Congress party has become a political party whether I liked it or not. The constitution is being drafted based on foreign models whether I liked it or not. Therefore, I have decided to take some remedial steps to fulfil my promises to the people. If by any chance, the two letters which I have addressed to Panditji did not bring the desired changes in him, please guide the young man to form the new political party – JANATA CONGRESS. Be its first chief servant. Let there be no name like President, Secretary etc for the party posts. All are to be known as Sewaks or servants. Please go through the constitutional model of Chandru which is tailor made for a country, which has just been released from the clutches of the foreigners for 700 years and more.

Further Chandru has a check list ready for immediate implementation to be taken by the new government formed after the election. If only you stand by him and help him to implement his check listed programs, plans, rules and regulations, besides the constitution, I am sure that every Indian would be guaranteed his share of the freedom. Chandru's constitution is better than communism, better than socialism, and allows the capitalism to exist side by side. We need such a strong base to construct the future of the nation.

In case, for reasons known to you, you are not able to join the new party, please do not worry. Chandru would accomplish the task, of course with out you, he has to take some more efforts. But I request you not to obstruct him or trouble him or stop him or discourage him in his efforts to complete the task. That is a favour I seek from you, in the name of our long association during the freedom movement. Jai Hind"

Both Chandru and Patel were sitting with out exchanging a word- for half an hour, when his daughter came to find out what her father doing in the guest's room.

"Officers from Home department are waiting for you ,papa" she announced and had gone.

Patel immediately left the room and after wards Chandru did not see him, till late evening.

Around 9 pm, suddenly Chandru heard taps on his room door. He went and opened the teak wood ornamental door. There he saw Patel followed by many senior leaders from congress. They all wished Chandru who reciprocated their greetings.

When every one was seated, Chandru was standing. Patel, shouted at him, " Betae, if I see you standing next time, I would get angry. Come and take your seat. All are our friends here. I have talked to every one personally and explained everything about you, and out Babuji's task. They have pledged their life for establishing the Ram Rajya with you as the leader, advisor or the first servant in the words of Mahatma. They are my good friends who tried their level best to make me as the President of the Congress twice and almost succeeded. But reasons, let us discuss, now, were there for me to step down .

Now, I am introducing them one by one to you . They are the Pradesh congress committee presidents from the provinces. They are also not happy with the changes that has been taking place after the impendence. They are the staunch supporters of Gandhiji's ideas of starting the new government from the villages. Now, you have to explain to them how what you would do if you form the government after successfully winning the majority in the parliament election. It is our duty and job to put you on top of the government. Now tell them. In the mean time I would make arrangements for our food "- left Chandru to handle the crowd of supporters.

Chandru looked around the crowd of sixteen senior congress men sitting in the available places, eagerly waiting to hear him. He then remembered Gandhiji once and prayed to his 'Ba' the source of his political inspiration and then softly commenced his maiden talk before party men.

" My dear friends, I can speak in Hindi as well in English- can I continue in English ?" he asked. Majority wanted Hindi only and hence Chandru began in ordinary conversational Hindi (for the purpose of the this book- the English translation is given here)

" My first duty is to thank you for joining us for making the dreams of our Mahatma come true. Secondly, I am ever indebted to Patel Saheb for providing me an opportunity to do my best for the country at the initial stages. With the support of **a man of steel**, we can any challenge and task. I must than k Gandhiji for having handed over me to Patel Saheb.

Now, I would like to make it clear at the outset,-political party is not a professional platform for personal enrichment not it is an opportunity to exercise powers or not it is an arena where one can fight to finish the opponents. The very objective of the government once fulfilled, the political parties should be dissolved and only systems should govern the country- before which all are equal and individual identity would be merged with the national identity.

As on date, the conditions prevailing are tricky. We have two different group of Indians- the one who has been perennially suffering for centuries- at the village levels- for whom, whether Congress ruled or JANATA congress ruled, it does not matter. They are called statistical Indians. The other group has been affluent-semi-affluent or on the threshold of affluence. They form the middle, upper middle and upper class. The country's present identity is contributed by them. With out them, our Country would have been listed with the land of aborigines in Africa or elsewhere in the globe. Only they wanted freedom as they only knew what was meant by freedom to a country. They are educated persons or people with very good common sense- they are found every where forming the minority but remaining at the top layer of the society. They neither like the monarchy nor the British dominance in their land. They feel that they are born to rule the country – country in the sense the people in it – people in the sense- those who have been suffering and putting up with all their day to day problems working like slaves for centuries .

There appears to be no change in the policies of those educated class who have initiated the struggle against the British way back in 19th century. Today, the interim government has taken over from the British and what we see – only the members of the educated aristocratic, upper, upper middle and middle class are holding charge of the ministries, and how many of them have gone to see the conditions of the villagers, forming the majority of the population, before functioning as the ministers? Please tell. They are sitting in big palaces, spacious decorated comfortable chambers talking about foreign models of constitution. Do you think that they can ever take up the cause of the poor majority? I doubt.

If by chance, we succeed in our efforts to form the first government, the very first thing, we should do to free the villagers from their perennial debts- to allow them to breathe the fresh air of freedom. For those poor millions, freedom is not industrial development, high-raising buildings, revolution in agricultural operations, improving the relationship with other countries, or entertaining foreign diplomats or visiting other countries , providing good transport facilities, ship building, air services, vehicle production, modernising communication etc. Those are for augmenting the comforts of the minority at the cost of the majority.

A villager who has not taken a square meal in his life, who has never seen a toilet with flush, who has never worn a dress which is not worn out, who has never slept under a roof which does not leak during the rains, who has never seen an electric light, who has never sent his children to school, who can never afford a good medial treatment, he should be the first in the agenda of the new government's action plan. Otherwise, the hope of taking up the case of those villagers is lost for ever. Now or never is the situation now. Once the government starts implementing their plans, keeping the middle class and above at the first beneficiaries, thereafter, they can take a 'U' turn and comeback to uplift the poor. By then much water would have flown under the bridge and no middle class group, would watch the government diverting their attention to the unfortunate poor villagers. By the time government decides to change their course of action, the middle class and above would have established their representatives in all key positions in the political party as well as in the governments and see to that only a notional or a token assistance is made to the poor. I even doubt that the leaders might make very big promises to do this and that to the gullible poor and after winning the elections might continue their loyalty to the middle and above classes.

Hence, if we succeed in forming the government, the very first thing I would do is to promulgate certain rules and regulations to start with, which would become the first step for addressing the problems of the poor who have been suffering with out respite for thousands of years. I have got everything ready- the acts to be promulgated, the check list of administrative reforms,. The new Indian constitution , the new criminal law, the new civil law, the election procedures, police reforms, legal procedures, development of education, medical facilities, industrial policies, tax laws, religion, sports, etc are just ready for implementation after they are enacted in the parliament. They all repeal the existing systems which suited the British and the educated middle class and above only. Hence entire working of the government machinery would be made-villager-friendly.   Every Indian whether illiterate or not, would be made to know the legal provisions and the essential provisions of the constitution.

No one would be allowed to say in India, with 90 % illiteracy- "ignorance of law is not an excuse". Let us teach the law to the poor before implementing them . Let us make them understand the provision of the constitution before enforcing them Let us think of the middle class and above, after providing food, shelter, water and clothing to the majority before worrying about the already well-off minority Indians. Jai Hind"

When Chandru finished his thought provoking and scintillating speech for the private audience, the first claps came from Patel who was standing at the threshold, hearing every word of what Chandru said.

He came almost running to hug Chandru and said loudly, " no wonder, my friend and soul mate, Gandhiji called him a political genius. "

"Betae, I have decided. Earlier there was a lurking doubt deep in my mind about you and about what Gandhiji has written about you. Now, I declare that I am with this visionary to build the modern India after independence."

When he raised his hand and shouted "Vande Mathram" all those who were present automatically stood up and chanted the same words. They then came and shook hands with Chandru and Patel, saying that they were eagerly waiting only for the launching the party.

www.ingramcontent.com/pod-product-compliance
Lightning Source LLC
Chambersburg PA
CBHW071227280526
45787CB00002B/838